ONE OF the most harrowing experiences for First World War soldiers was the Battle of the Somme. From July to November, 1916, British, French and German troops struggled for control of a part of the Western Front straddling the River Somme in France. The Battle began under the summer skies of July and was heralded by Britain and France as the breakthrough that would end the stalemate of trench warfare. It finished in a sea of mud with the German line still unbroken, and over a million casualties to show for the few, devastated miles "won" by the Allies.

The author describes the notorious first attack of the Battle, on 1st July, when the New Armies of 1914 volunteers first saw large-scale action. Sixty thousand men were mown down by German machine guns in one of the greatest British military disasters. The haunting names of the villages and woods, which were the German strongpoints in the area, are engraved on war memorials throughout Britain. Christopher Martin shows how the Battle, which was the mid-point of the war, was a microcosm of the whole conflict, moving from crusade-like zest to bitter disillusionment. It also marked the beginning of modern warfare: the first tanks and the first effective fighting aeroplanes went into action alongside cavalrymen armed with lances.

The author points out the striking difference between the two kinds of sources recounting the Battle. First, the official statements of Army and Government, elaborated by the Press to celebrate an epic "victory." And, in poignant contrast, the unofficial comments in letters, diaries, memoirs, novels and poems by fighting soldiers, who record the human drama and nightmare landscapes of the Somme, and reveal "what kind of a bestial horror the war has become."

Battle of the Somme

Christopher Martin

As they marched through one little village, at about ten o'clock,
doors suddenly opened and light fell through the doorways, and
voices asked them where they were going.

"Somme! Somme!" they shouted as though it were a challenge.

"Ah, no bon!" came the kindly, pitying voices in reply; and
even after the doors closed again, and they had left that village
behind, the kindly voices seemed to drift across the darkness,
like the voices of ghosts: "Somme! Ah, no bon!"

Frederic Manning, *Her Privates We*

1916
The world bloodily minded,
The church dead or polluted,
The blind leading the blinded,
And the deaf dragging the muted.
Israel Zangwill

WAYLAND PUBLISHERS · LONDON

Frontispiece A street shrine to local war casualties in the East End of London, 1916

SBN 85340 308 2
Copyright © 1973 by Wayland (Publishers) Ltd
101 Grays Inn Road, London WC1
Set in 'Monophoto' Times and printed offset litho in Great Britain by
Page Bros (Norwich) Ltd, Norwich

Contents

The Illustrations

1 The Call to Arms

WAR CAME SUDDENLY to Europe in August, 1914. For the past decade, the two great alliances that divided the continent – Germany and Austria–Hungary against France, Russia and Britain – had nearly come to blows over disputed "spheres of influence," or over colonial and trade rivalry. France still resented the loss of Alsace-Lorraine in the 1870 Franco–Prussian war; Austria–Hungary and Russia struggled for control of the Balkan States; Britain and Germany jealously regarded each other's colonial expansion. In the summer of 1914, although tensions seemed to have decreased, these old rivalries were enough to carry the Continent to war. "The fundamental causes of the conflict can be epitomized in three words – fear, hunger, pride," wrote the historian, B. H. Liddell-Hart. "Beside them the international incidents that occurred between 1871 and 1914 are but symptoms (1)."

The coming of war

Fear had created huge armies and navies and elaborate plans for war. In this explosive atmosphere, the spark of the assassination of Archduke Franz Ferdinand, in June, 1914, at Sarajevo in Bosnia, was enough to cause a final explosion. The Archduke was heir to the throne of Austria–Hungary; his assassins were supposedly helped by Serbia, Russia's ally. The tragic sequence of declarations of war among the great powers, begun only as diplomatic bluff, followed from 28th July to 2nd August. "Fifty years were spent in the process of making Europe explosive," went on Liddell-Hart. "Five days were enough to detonate it (2)."

Britain became involved when the German armies, on their way to France, entered Belgium, whose neutrality was guaran-

Britain declares war   9

Opposite Tommy Atkins leaves his family to "do his bit" as a Kitchener volunteer

teed by international treaty. It was this "scrap of paper" that made Britain declare war on Germany on 4th August. The attack on Belgium – that John Galsworthy, the novelist, called "this most gallant of little countries ground because of sheer loyalty beneath an iron heel (3)," seemed to most British people to justify the declaration. Excited crowds in London, here described by *The Times* correspondent, Michael Macdonagh, greeted the outbreak: "There was no public proclamation that we were at war by a herald to the sound of trumpets and beating of drums. The great crowd rapidly dispersed in all directions, most of them running to get home quickly and as they ran they cried aloud rather hysterically, 'War! War! War!' (4)"

Reactions to war
Certainly the war seemed a relief for the pent-up tensions of the last decade. The Prime Minister's son, Herbert Asquith, compared the coming of war to the release of stagnant waters from a dam (5).

> *The clouds roll back, the breadth of heaven clears.*
> *Those tired and darkening waters in the lock*
> *Foam out, a flood of silver, down the weirs,*
> *And tear the moss from faces of the rocks.*

His friend, Rupert Brooke, caught the national mood in these famous lines (6):

> *Now God be thanked who has matched us with his hour,*
> *And caught our youth, and wakened us from sleeping,*
> *With hand made sure, clear eye, and sharpened power,*
> *To turn, as swimmers into cleanness leaping,*
> *Glad from a world grown old and cold and weary . . .*

Lord Kitchener's insight
Leading opinion felt that it would be a short war, "over by Christmas." Britain's small Army Expeditionary Force of seven divisions was at once sent to France. It was thought the Force would be sufficient to allow Britain to play an honourable part in the land battles, while her Navy crushed all rivals at sea. Lord Kitchener, Secretary of State for War, had a long practical experience of war in Africa, which gave him more insight into the conflict than many of his contemporaries. Winston Churchill reported Kitchener's speech to the Cabinet. "Everyone expected that the war would be short but wars took unexpected courses

and we must now prepare for a long struggle. Such a conflict would not be ended . . . by sea power alone. It could only be ended by great battles on the Continent. In these the British Empire must bear its part on a scale proportionate to its magnitude and power. We must be prepared to put armies of millions in the field and to maintain them for several years (7)."

Britain, unlike Continental powers who had huge conscript armies, had relied on a small regular army. The army was supplemented by territorials, who were part-time volunteer soldiers. So this plan for "armies of millions" was a revolution in military thinking. Kitchener pressed forward with his "gigantic experiment." On 6th August, his first general appeal was published in the newspapers. *The call to arms*

"YOUR KING AND COUNTRY NEED YOU.

A call to Arms.

"An addition of 100,000 men to His Majesty's Regular Army is immediately necessary in the present grave National Emergency. Lord Kitchener is confident that this appeal will be at once responded to by all who have the safety of our Empire at heart . . .

GOD SAVE THE KING."

Pressures were brought to bear on young men of military age. For such propaganda, the poster was the most striking way of convincing men to enlist. A Parliamentary Recruiting Committee commissioned a series of poster designs, among which two were outstanding: Alfred Leete's drawing of the pointing Kitchener, and the notorious "Daddy, what did you do in the Great War?" *War posters*

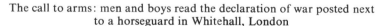

The call to arms: men and boys read the declaration of war posted next to a horseguard in Whitehall, London

designed to shame men into the Army. Michael Macdonagh, *The Times* correspondent, reported: "The town [London] is vibrant with the call to arms. Posters appealing for recruits are to be seen on every hoarding, in most shop windows, on omnibuses, tramcars and commercial vehicles. The great base of the Nelson pillar is covered with them, . . . several recruiting posters of a novel kind here have just appeared on the walls, . . . one is addressed to 'the young women of London.' It runs 'Is your best boy wearing khaki? If not, don't you think he should be?'

" 'If he does not think that you and your country are worth fighting for – do you think he is worthy of you?'

" 'Don't pity the girl who is alone: her young man is probably a soldier, fighting for her and his country and for you (8).' "

The White Feather Campaign

It was everyone's duty to "do his bit." "Shirkers" were relentlessly pursued. The White Feather campaign aimed to persuade "cowardly" young men to join up. Macdonagh described how this worked: "Going home in a tramcar the other night I was witness of the presentation of a white feather. The victims were two young men who were rudely disturbed from their reading of the evening paper by the attack of three young women. 'Why don't you fellows enlist? Your King and Country want you!' 'We don't!' One of the girls was a pretty wench. She dishonoured one of the young men . . . by sticking a white feather in his buttonhole, and a look of contempt spoiled for a moment her pretty face (9)."

The mood of the volunteers

A flood of men came forward: the total of 3,000 recorded on 9th August had swelled to 30,000 a day by the end of August as news from France grew blacker. Kitchener's famous phrases – "The First Hundred Thousand," "The New Armies," "This is a young man's war" – caught the public imagination. The writer J. B. Priestley, who was a volunteer soldier, described the zest of that time: "There came, out of the unclouded blue of that summer, a challenge that was almost like a conscription of the spirit, little to do really with King and country and flag-waving and hip-hip-hoorah, a challenge to what we felt was our untested manhood. Other men, who had not lived as easily as we had, had drilled and marched and borne arms – couldn't we? Yes, we too could leave home and soft beds and the girls to soldier for a spell, if there was

Opposite Some of the many posters commissioned by the Parliamentary Recruiting Committee in 1914

Daddy, what did _YOU_ do in the Great War?

"YOUR COUNTRY NEEDS YOU"

STEP INTO YOUR PLACE

some excuse for it, something at least to be defended. And here it it was . . . (10)"

Men from all walks of life volunteered. The popular writer Ian Hay caught their variety and motives in the preface to *The First Hundred Thousand* (11).

> *But yesterday, we said farewell*
> *to plough; to pit; to dock; to mill.*
> *For glory? Drop it! Why? Oh, well –*
> *To have a slap at Kaiser Bill.*
>
> *And now today has come along.*
> *With rifle, haversack and pack,*
> *We're off, a hundred thousand strong*
> *And – some of us will not come back.*
>
> *But all we ask, if that befall,*
> *Is this. Within your hearts be writ*
> *This single line memorial –*
> *He did his duty – and his bit!*

Joining the army

The recruiting sergeants took thousands under age. One of them was George Coppard. "The sergeant asked me my age, and, when told, replied, 'Clear off, son. Come back tomorrow and see if you're nineteen, eh?' So I turned up again next day and gave my age as nineteen. I attested in a bunch of a dozen others, and, holding up my right hand, swore to fight for King and country. The sergeant winked as he gave me the King's shilling . . . (12)"

The "Pals" battalions

The volunteers were attached, as "service battalions" of about a thousand men, to the existing regimental structure of the army. The famous "Pals" battalions, started in Liverpool, were groups of men of similar jobs who volunteered together. They were remarkable for their spirit. A Liverpool local paper reported their march through the city. "There was no vain glory about this display . . . there was just the tramp, tramp, of smart, well set-up young gentlemen, shoulders thrown back and faces stern and resolute, denoting a determination to go forward with a duty in the cause of civilization (13)." The Pals battalions, formed in many industrial towns, were among the most tragic casualties of the first Somme attack: the men of whole communities were mown down together on 1st July, 1916.

At the other end of the social scale, a society lady organized

New Army volunteers taking the oath in August, 1914

two "sportsmen's battalions" of "upper and middle class men, physically fit, able to shoot and ride." They formed a unique group. "In one hut . . . the first bed was occupied by the brother of a peer, the second by the man who drove his car . . . Other beds were occupied by a mechanical engineer, an old Blundell school boy, planters, a mine overseer from Scotland, a man in possession of a flying pilot certificate issued in France, an old sea-dog who had rounded Cape Horn on no fewer than nine occasions, a man who had hunted seals 'with more patches on his trousers than he could count' . . . (14)"

By the end of September, three-quarters of a million men had enlisted. By March, 1916, when conscription began, two and a half million men had volunteered. They formed the five New Armies, that would see action in Flanders, France and the Middle East. In particular, many were destined for the Somme. *The New Armies*

Not everyone approved of the mushrooming New Armies. Sir Henry Wilson, a well-known General, wrote to Winston Churchill about "[Kitchener's] shadow armies for shadow campaigns . . . *Regular army disapproval*

15

Under no circumstances can these mobs now being raised . . . take the field for two years. Then what is the use of them?" Kitchener's "ridiculous and preposterous army" was "the laughing stock of every soldier in Europe (15)."

Lack of uniforms

There were more reasoned criticisms to be made: skilled workers were not weeded out; lack of weapons and instructors meant that recruits received an incomplete training. Most disappointing for the men was the lack of uniforms. Civilian dress became military by stages. One battalion received old scarlet jackets from the 1890s; another man was reported dressed in a "bowler hat, khaki jacket, blue trousers and smart brown boots." Macdonagh attended a New Army inspection in September. "The third division presented a ludicrous spectacle, so motley was their array as they marched past the King . . . Some were only half made up, wearing scarlet jackets, the kilts or the trews of the old army uniform mingled with articles of civilian attire, all in glaring contrast. Some again wore a sort of provisional uniform of blue serge, suggesting inmates of prisons or hospitals . . . There was . . . a diversified and discordant display of straw hats, bowlers and tweed caps. And many were armed with staves. What particularly interested me . . . was the sight of many wearers of top hats, frock coats and spatted boots – lion hearts beating under the height of fashion. Others had the appearance of tramps. But . . . they were all bravely carrying on with a determination to become soldiers (16)."

Indian army officers on leave, retired officers, "dugouts" who had fought in half-forgotten Victorian campaigns were put in charge, with the handful of B.E.F. Regulars directed to stay home. Temporary commissions were granted to young men with Officers Training Corps experience. If expertise was lacking in the instruction, enthusiasm was not. "The voice of the drill sergeant is to be heard from morning until night in the Royal Parks, the gardens of the Inns of Court and in several of the squares," reported Macdonagh (17).

Pleasures of New Army life

Few soldiers anticipated what trench warfare would be like. The days were spent in drill, marching and digging. The new health, the open air, the comradeship made these happy days for many men. "The mental peace, the physical joy, the divinely

16

simplified sense of having one clear aim," were pleasures of the new life recalled by the journalist, C. E. Montague. "Always to have just some one and not hard thing to do; to be free to give yourself up . . . to whole days of rude health; to let yourself go with a will in the swing of the marching . . . (18)"

Montague vividly expressed the brief mood of crusade that motivated the volunteers. "Who will not remember until he dies the second boyhood that he had in the late frosts and then in the swiftly filling and bursting spring and early summer of 1915? The awakening bird notes of reveilles at dawn, the two mile run through the auroral mists breaking over a still inviolate England, the men's smoking breath and the swish of their feet brushing the dew from the tips of the June grass and printing their track of darker green on the pearly-gray turf; the long, intent morning parades under the gummy shine of chestnut buds in the deepening meadows . . . and then jocund days of marching and digging trenches in the sun, the silly little songs on the road . . . The dinners of haversack rations you ate as you sat on the road-makers' heaps of chopped stones or lay back among the butter-cups (19)."

Significantly Montague's book is called *Disenchantment*. The idealism of Kitchener's New Armies was doomed to perish in the Somme carnage. In 1919 an officer wrote to *The Nation*, a weekly magazine, recalling the days of 1914. "We were happy that our country had gone to war . . . We were going to do great things for one another and for the folks at home. We were going to win fame and glory . . . We really believed that we were going to fight for freedom, as the press and government told us . . . (20)" That was the dream. In the bungled actions and drab misery of the trenches it was lost.

Hopes of the New Army

2 "Out There":
The Soldier's Life in France

THE WESTERN FRONT was a continuous line of trenches stretching 450 miles from the Swiss border to the Belgian coast. It was born from the failure of the German plan for a quick victory over France. The Schlieffen plan (designed in 1905 by the German Army Staff) was a rapid German sweep through Belgium and Northern France that would capture Paris and surround the French armies. But in September, 1914, the Allies held and pushed back this German thrust at the River Marne in France. The Germans retreated and dug trenches along the Aisne. As both sides scrambled northward in the "race to the sea," the lines were extended. During the winter of 1914–15, as the exhausted armies rebuilt their strength, the trenches became a complex of ditches, stretching for mile after mile.

The Western Front

Trenches had been used in earlier wars as a temporary measure, but in 1915 the quick-firing gun and barbed wire made them seem permanent. The defence was now far stronger than any attacker. In 1900 a French military expert, Ivan Bloch, had shrewdly foretold: "Everybody will be entrenched in the next war . . . The spade will be as indispensable to a soldier as his rifle . . . The war . . . will become a kind of stalemate, in which, neither army being able to get at the other, both armies will be maintained in opposition to each other, threatening each other but never able to deliver a final and decisive attack (21)."

Trenches

The Western Front became an impregnable barrier, which the novelist Henry Williamson described as "that great livid wound that lay across Europe, suppurating during more than fifteen hundred nights and days – torrents of steel and prairie fires

Opposite British troops carry up rations to the front trenches, 1st July, 1916

19

of flame . . . (22)" To this bizarre tangle of ditches, millions of men were drawn; it became what the poet Siegfried Sassoon called "the hell where youth and laughter go."

Despite the plea of an imaginative soldier like Kitchener that "the German lines in France may be looked on as a fortress that cannot be carried by assault (23)," the Allied generals went on hurling attacks at the wall. They were "content to fight machine gun bullets with the breasts of gallant men (24)." The Battle of the Somme was to be one such attempted breakthrough.

The "Old Front Line" By the spring of 1916, the British held, as their share of the Front, some eighty miles of trenches from Ypres to the River Somme. This was the "Old Front Line." Ypres was the focus of British effort; once a beautiful medieval town, it was now "a wilderness of looped and windowed walls (25)." "Wipers," wrote the novelist Henry Williamson, using the soldiers' slang name, "with the sun on it, looked like the long white jawbone of a mule, with its teeth chipped and splintered (26)." The Line then passed across the grim Artois plain where the battle failures of 1915, like Neuve Chapelle and Loos, were fought among slagheaps and mining villages. Then it crossed the rolling chalk hills of Picardy where the trenches showed as a tangle of white lines on the downland.

Old soldiers As he stood on the ship crossing the channel, the soldier newcomer to France might first be impressed by experienced trench soldiers returning after leave. The novelist, Richard Aldington, described them. "The leave men were dressed anyhow . . . Some wore overcoats, some shaggy goatskin or rough sheepskin jackets. The skirts of some overcoats had been roughly hacked off with jack knives – not to trail in the deep mud . . The bolts and muzzles of their rifles were generally tightly bound with oiled rags . . . their faces . . . were lean and still curiously drawn although the men had been out of the line for a fortnight; the eyes had a peculiar look. They seemed strangely worn and mature but filled with energy (27)."

Training camps Active service began at the base camps on the coast. A soldier often had his first taste of war atmosphere in such grim arenas as "The Bull Ring" at Etaples, "that thirsty, savage, interminable training ground (28)." Although the bayonet was actually little

.303 Lee Enfield rifle and
bayonet
2 gas helmets and goggles
220 rounds of rifle
ammunition
2 mills grenades
2 empty sandbags
Pair of wire cutters
Entrenching tool
A flare
Steel helmet
Field dressing and iodine
Belt for bayonet
Water bottle
Groundsheet
Haversack
Mess tin and food
Spare socks
"Housewife" sewing kit
Note also putees round
calf (A survival from
fighting in India, used as a
protection against snakes)

The uniform and equipment of British soldiers on the Somme

used in action, the instructors felt it was useful to create "The Spirit of the Offensive." Philip Gibbs, a journalist, described the spectacle. The soldiers "lunged at the hanging sacks, stabbing them where the red circles were painted. These inanimate things became revoltingly life-like as they jerked to and fro . . . one fell from a rope and a boy sprang at it, dug his bayonet in, put his foot on the prostrate thing to get a purchase for his bayonet which he lugged out again and then kicked the sack (29)."

Col. Ronald Campbell, who gave celebrated lectures on "the Spirit of the Bayonet," conveyed the brutal mood of the training camps. "You've got to get down and hook them out with the bayonet; you will enjoy that, I can assure you (laughter) . . . The only time that a German can find pluck to kill with the bayonet is when he comes across one of our own wounded; he will plunge the steel into their hearts as they lie unable to defend themselves. When you see this done, can you have any sympathy for them?

*The "Spirit of
the Bayonet"*

21

No! Ten thousand times no! Kill them, every mother's son of them! Remember that your job is to kill them – that is the only way – exterminate the vile creatures! (30)"

Journey to the trenches
The soldiers began the journey to the trenches with a slow train ride to "rail head" in freight trucks. A night arrival was the most spectacular, as Richard Aldington described. "Once again the train started and crawled interminably . . . Then . . . came a much nearer and brighter flash, followed almost at once by a deep boom audible above the noise of the train. The other men heard it this time: 'The guns!' (31)"

Artillery
The final stage of the journey towards that horizon "faintly reverberating, glowing fitfully, trembling with light (32)" was on foot. The gun batteries marked the outer limits of the battle-zone. The firing of the guns was awesome enough for a newcomer. The soldier artist P. Wyndham-Lewis remembered. "Very suddenly there was a flash near at hand . . . they appeared to be 11 inch guns – very big . . . out of their throats had sprung a dramatic flame, they had roared, they had moved back. You could see them, lighted from their mouths as they hurled into the air their great projectiles and sank back as they did it (33)."

Far worse was the first taste of enemy shell fire. The soldiers made their way to the front through communication trenches that began well behind the firing trench. As they usually moved at night, the journey was difficult. John Masefield, the poet, described some of the men's feelings. "Many men . . . as they went 'in' for the first time, felt with a sinking of the heart, that they were leaving all ordered and arranged things, perhaps for ever . . . (34)" They passed dugouts where candlelight gleamed beyond sacking doors, or groups of mudstained men huddled round a brazier. They went forward "following the load on the back of the man in front, the black walls of the trench, and now and then some gleam of a star in the water underfoot. Sometimes as they marched they would see the starshells; going up and bursting like rockets, and coming down . . . as white and bright as burning magnesium . . . (35)"

In the trenches
In daylight the newcomer could sort out the maze of earth passages with their homely English names. The "ideal trench" was six feet deep with parapets of sandbags to absorb rifle bullets,

fire steps for sentries and duckboards over drainage channels. But these were rare. Most men in the front line "lived" in shallow holes cut in the side of the trench; the officers used an old cellar or some deeper burrow. "There were mascots, for luck, at the doorways of their dugouts," wrote the journalist Philip Gibbs, "a woman's face carved in chalk, the name of a girl written in pebbles, a portrait of the King in a frame of withered flowers (36)." It was a primitive way of life. Gibbs went on, "They lived in a world which is as different from this known world of ours as though they belonged to another race of men inhabiting another planet, or to an old race far back behind the memory of the first civilization (37)."

It was hard to keep the trenches dry or free of vermin. Gibbs described the natural horrors. "The water through which we waded was alive with a multitude of swimming frogs. Red slugs crawled up the sides of the trenches, and queer beetles with dangerous looking horns wriggled along dry ledges and invaded the dugouts in search of the vermin which infested them.

"'Rats are the worst plague,' said a colonel . . . 'There are thousands of rats in this part of the line and they're audacious devils. In the dugout next door the straw at night writhes with them (38).'"

There were other horrors. Corpses of men became imbedded into the ground they had defended. "At some points in the trench, bones pierced through their shallow burial, and skulls appeared like mushrooms (39)," reported the poet, Edmund Blunden. George Coppard remembered, "Every square yard of ground seemed to be layered with corpses, producing a sickening stench. We would curtain off protruding parts with a sandbag, pinned to the side of the trench with cartridges. A swollen right arm, with a German eagle tattooed on it, used to stick out and brush us as we squeezed by, and once a head appeared which wasn't there an hour before . . . (40)"

The trench smell was described by the poet Robert Graves as "compounded of stagnant mud, latrine buckets, chloride of lime, unburied and half-buried corpses, rotting sandbags, stale human sweat, fumes of cordite and lyddite. Sometimes it was sweetened by cigarette smoke and the scent of bacon frying over wood fires;

Horrors of the trenches

Trench smell

23

sometimes made sinister by the lingering odour of poison gas (41)."

"No Man's Land" If a soldier cast a furtive glance over the parapet into "No Man's Land" between the trench lines he might see "the same old sandbags in the enemy's line . . . the blasted tree sliced by shell fire, the upturned railway truck of which only the metal remained, the distant fringe of trees like gallows on the skyline (42)."

Daily routine The daily routine of trench life was opposite to normal life: night was the time for work; day was for resting. Dawn and dusk were marked by "stand-to," when all men lined the parapet in case of attack. After dusk, the real work began. Carrying "fatigues" brought up trench supplies from the rear. Charles Carrington, a line officer, remembered the variety of loads: "Dry rations made up in bundles . . . trench stores – planks, pit-props, duckboards, coils of barbed wire, sandbags in bales; boxes of rifle ammunition and Mills bombs; gallon jars of rum . . . the mail . . . water medicated with chloride of lime and tasting of the petrol cans in which it was carried; there was hot stew in two gallon 'dixies' . . . (43)"

Trench patrols The men dreaded the "wiring-parties," fatigues that went out to repair the day's damage to the barbed wire. There were also patrols that prowled into No-Man's land to explore or to raid the enemy's trenches. Robert Graves described the nightmares there: "Once I snatched my fingers in horror from where I had planted them on the slimy body of an old corpse . . . Many of the craters contained the corpses of men who had been wounded and crept in there to die. Some were skeletons picked clean by the rats (44)."

Miseries of trench life During the day, the men rested uneasily. They remained fully dressed throughout the trench tour of three to four days, with rifles ready beside them. Rarely did a day pass, even in "quiet" areas, without a casualty or an alarm. In winter, rain and cold were unspeakable miseries. Boredom was another, as Philip Gibbs saw.

"'What casualties?' asked the adjutant in his dugout.

"'Two killed, three wounded, sir!'

"'Very well . . . you can go.'

"A salute in the doorway of the dugout, a groan from the adjutant lighting another cigarette, leaning with his elbows on the

24

Opposite An officer leads his men "over the top" on a trench raid

deal table, staring at the guttering of the candle by his side, at the pile of forms in front of him, at the glint of light on a steel helmet hanging by its strap on a nail, near the shelf where he kept his safety razor, flashlamp, love letters (in an old cigar box), soap, whisky bottle (almost empty now) and an unread novel. "'Hell! What a life!' (45)"

Meals   Meals were monotonous – ration biscuits, bread, tinned meat, "plum and apple" jam. There were cigarettes and a daily ration of thick strong rum, and a hot meal, perhaps, at dusk. Trench life proved strangely healthy, except for "trench feet," caused by constant damp that turned the feet green and swollen, and the lice which infested all front line soldiers.

Discipline   Trench discipline was stern. "Field Punishment Number One" was a humiliation. The offender was "crucified" – tied with arms outstretched to a cartwheel for two hours at a time. Death sentences might be given for desertion or cowardice, although only 346 men actually died in this way.

Weapons   The weapons of the trench war were dominated by the mighty artillery. What the poet, Wilfred Owen, called "the monstrous anger of the guns" could be heard clearly in England. Gilbert Frankau, an artillery officer, wrote (46):

We are the guns, and your masters! Saw ye our flashes?
Heard ye the scream of our shells in the night and the shuddering crashes?
Saw ye our work at the roadside, the shrouded things lying,
Moaning to God that he made them, the maimed and the dying?
Husbands or sons,
Fathers or lovers, we break them. We are the Guns!

The small fieldguns, firing "Whizzbangs" with a flat trajectory, were less dangerous than the howitzers. These guns were placed further back and hurled a shell upward in a curving flight. Such shells could enter and shatter a trench. The artillery was the crude hammer to begin an attack, but it could also be employed in defence.

Machine guns   The machine gun, "the concentrated essence of infantry" with its destructive fire power, was the key to the stalemate of the Western Front. The journalist, H. M. Tomlinson, noted its effect in the increasing mechanization of war. "As things are . . . a consumptive machine-gunner . . . can sit in a lucky hole in the ground and scupper a company of the best as they advance. Courage isn't what it used to be. The machine runs over us and we can't stop it (47)."

Other weapons were invented or rediscovered from past wars as a result of the conditions of trench fighting. Poison gas and the flame-thrower were terrible newcomers to battle; the bomb, the mortar, the tunnel mine packed with high explosives to blow up enemy strongpoints, were recalled from the Crimea. Until the tank, nothing dealt effectively with barbed wire. The statistics recording causes of wounds among British troops show how effective the weapons were: Shell/trench mortar 58%; Rifle/machine gun 39%; Bombs and grenades 2·19%; Bayonet 0·32%.

New inventions

About sixty men became casualties in a battalion each month between the great battles. The soldiers envied those who had "Blighty" wounds, just serious enough to transfer a man to England. Some desperate men wounded themselves. Death, when it came, swooped suddenly out of the air, as the poet Edmund Blunden recorded. "Soon a cry from that place recalled me; the shell had burst all wrong. Its butting impression was black and stinking on the parados where three minutes ago, the lance corporal's mess tin was bubbling over a little flame. For him, how could the gobbets of blackening flesh, the earth wall sotted with blood, with flesh, the eye under the duckboard, the pulpy bone be the only answer? (48)"

Close bonds of comradeship were formed out of the shared suffering of trench life, "a generous warmth, even nobility engendered among quite ordinary men at the front (49)." An officer, Roland Fielding, wrote to his wife, "In spite of . . . the gloominess of the surroundings, there was an atmosphere of selflessness . . . the like of which has probably not been seen in the world before . . . Such is the influence of the shells (50)." The loss of a comrade was the harshest blow to a man's morale. *The Nation* pointed this out in an article about the ordinary soldier. "The great spiritual bond in the army is that of comradeship. The loss of a 'pal' is the greatest sorrow a soldier suffers, and may deeply affect his spirits and character (51)."

Trench comradeship

The worst blow to a soldier's morale was the death of a comrade

The soldiers were usually transferred to other sectors of the Front on foot, as there was little mechanical transport. Along "those monotonous miles," the troops sang to the rhythm of their boots on the road. The novelist, Frederic Manning, recalled these famous songs. "The rhythm of all those tramping feet slurring the stresses slightly, held him in its curious hypnosis . . . The men sang, sang to keep up cheerful hearts.

> "Ere we are, 'ere we are, 'ere we are again,
> Pat, and Mack, and Tommy, and Jack, and Joe,
> Never mind the weather! Now then all together!
> Are we downhearted? No! ('ave a banana!)
> 'Ere we are, 'ere we are . . .'

"It might have gone on indefinitely but the men suddenly switched onto 'Cock Robin,' in which some voices would interject, 'another poor mother has lost her son' as though to affront the sinister fate against which they were determined to march with a swagger . . . (52)"

28

The historian, A. J. P. Taylor, thought of these songs as popular poetry: "The humble Englishman found his voice, and these songs preserve him for posterity (53)." A favourite of the Somme era was, in fact, composed by a professional song-writer (54):

There's a long, long trail a-winding
Into the land of my dreams,
Where the nightingales are singing
And a white moon beams.
There's a long, long night of waiting
Until my dreams all come true
Till the day that I'll be going
Down that long, long trail with you

The soldiers' happiest march was away from the trenches to a rest period in the rear area. Edmund Blunden wrote, "The joyful path away from the Line on that glittering summer morning was full of pictures for my infant war mind . . . Acres of self sown wheat glistened and sighed as we wound our way between . . . Life, life abundant sang here and smiled; the lizard ran warless in the warm dust, and the ditches were trembling quick with odd, tiny fish, in worlds as remote as Saturn . . . (55)"

For the lucky few, there might be leave to Britain itself. *Soldiers'* As the war went on, soldiers worn out by battle were increasingly *leave in* puzzled by the militant atmosphere in Britain. "England looked *Britain* strange to us returned soldiers," wrote Robert Graves. "We could not understand the war madness that ran wild everywhere, looking for a pseudo-military outlet. The civilians talked a foreign language, and it was newspaper language (56)."

The press distorted and romanticized the war. The writer R. H. *The Press* Tawney, then a volunteer N.C.O., wrote to *The Nation,* protest- *image* ing "There has been invented a kind of conventional soldier whose emotions and ideas are those which you find it most easy to assimilate with your coffee and marmalade. And this 'Tommy' is a creature at once ridiculous and disgusting. He is represented as invariably 'cheerful' and revelling in the 'excitement' of war, on finding 'sport' in killing other men, or hunting Germans out of dugouts as a terrier hunts rats . . . we are depicted as merry assassins rejoicing in the opportunity of a 'scrap' . . . exulting in the duty of turning human beings into lumps of disfigured clay . . . of

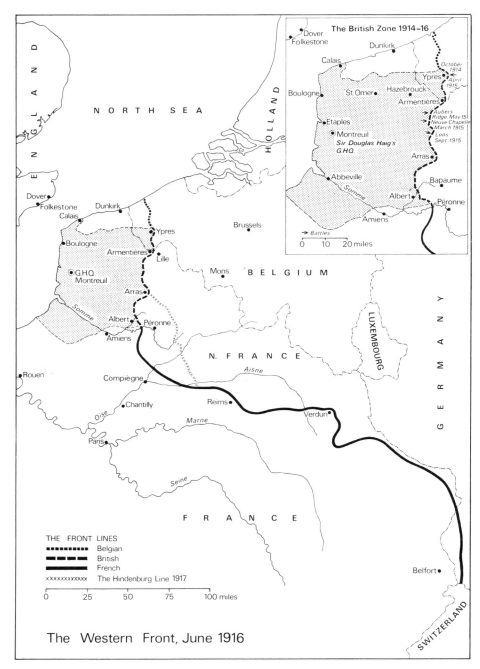

The British Zone 1914-16

Dover
Folkestone
Dunkirk
Calais
October 1914
Ypres
April 1915
Boulogne
St.Omer
Hazebrouck
Armentières
Etaples
Aubers Ridge.May 15
Neuve Chapelle March 1915
Loos Sept.1915
Montreuil
Sir Douglas Haig's G.H.Q.
Arras
Abbeville
Bapaume
Somme
Albert
Péronne
Amiens

→ Battles

0   10   20 miles

NORTH SEA

ENGLAND

HOLLAND

Dover
Folkestone
Calais
Dunkirk
Ypres
Brussels
Boulogne
Armentières
Lille
Mons
BELGIUM
G.H.Q.
Montreuil
Arras
Somme
Albert
Péronne
Amiens
N. FRANCE
Aisne
LUXEMBOURG
Rouen
Compiègne
Chantilly
Reims
Verdun
GERMANY
Oise
Marne
Paris
Seine
FRANCE

THE FRONT LINES

••••••••••	Belgian
▬ ▬ ▬ ▬	British
▬▬▬▬▬	French
xxxxxxxxxxxx	The Hindenburg Line 1917

0   25   50   75   100 miles

Belfort

SWITZERLAND

The Western Front, June 1916

30

Opposite Reconstructing enemy trenches from air photographs taken
by R.F.C. pilots

your soldier's internal life, the sensation of taking part in a game played by monkeys and organized by lunatics, you realize . . . nothing (57)."

There was also a new sort of warrior at the Front, the airmen of the Royal Flying Corps. Flying had developed rapidly because aircraft were valuable for reconnaissance behind enemy lines. The R.F.C. had a glamorous image, although the average life of a pilot at the front was only three weeks and his death was a sudden plunge to destruction. No parachutes were allowed. From the tented aerodromes behind the lines, the R.F.C. men flew to kill or be killed. Philip Gibbs felt their magic as he watched their aircraft leave. "When the sun rose, its rays touched their wings, made them white like cabbage butterflies, or changed them to silver, all a-sparkle (58)." *Airmen*

The fliers' lives were short, and strained to the utmost. Gibbs went on, "They became fatalists, after a few fights, and believed in their luck, or their mascots – Teddy Bears, a bullet that had missed them, china dolls, a girl's lock of hair, a silver ring. Yet at the back of their brains most of them, I fancy, knew that it was only a question of time before they 'went west' (59)."

Cecil Lewis, an "ace" pilot, described the departure of a squadron to France. "We stood on the tarmac, watching them go . . . They came hurtling up, their goggled pilots and observers leaning down to wave a last farewell before they passed in a deafening flash of speed and smoke fifty feet overhead. One by one they came up as if saluting us – drum roll crescendo, cymbal crash, rapid diminuendo . . . It was a prelude to action in that noble and tragic adventure of the world's youth . . . They were a symbol of the time, young men who rose up, passed with a cry and a gesture and were gone (60)."

3 "Blighty": Life in Wartime Britain

1916 MARKED the high tide mark of British enthusiasm for the war. The mood of the country up to 1916 was similar to that of civilians during the Napoleonic wars, as described by the poet Coleridge (61):

> *Secure from actual warfare, we have loved*
> *To swell the war whoop, passionate for war! . . .*
> *The which we pay for as a thing to talk of*
> *Spectators and not combatants . . .*
> *We send our mandates for the certain death*
> *Of thousands and ten thousands! Boys and girls*
> *And women, that would groan to see a child*
> *Pull off a insect's leg, all read or war,*
> *The best amusement for our morning meal! . . .*
> *As if the soldier died without a wound . . .*
> *As though he had no wife to pine for him . . .*

The severe losses in battle, and the hysterical tone of propaganda made the war fever of 1914–18 more sinister. The novelist, D. H. Lawrence, sensed in wartime London "a feeling of savagery in the air, the feeling of murder in the dark dreadful city." He wrote in a letter, "It seems as if we are all going to be dragged into the *danse macabre*. One can only grin and be fatalistic. My dear nation is bitten by the tarantula, and the venom has gone home at last. Now it is dance, *mes amis*, to the sound of the knuckle bones . . . (62)" His friend, Mark Gertler, the artist, painted an image of war fever in "The Merry-Go-Round," where war-crazed soldiers and civilians chant the slogans of coarse patriotism.

Opposite "The Merry-Go-Round" by Mark Gertler (1916): a picture of war fever

Busybodies found scope in the hunt for "shirkers," who stood aside while others toiled for the war effort. One woman, called the "Little Mother," wrote a celebrated letter to *The Morning Post* against the "pacifists" who sought a negotiated peace. "I say that we women . . . will tolerate no such cry as 'Peace! Peace!' where there is no peace. The corn that will wave over land watered by the blood of our brave lads shall testify to the future that their blood was not spilt in vain . . . In our homes at least there shall be no 'sitting at home warm and cosy in the winter, cool and comfy in the summer.' There is only one temperature for the women of British race, and that is white heat. With those who disgrace their sacred trust of motherhood we have nothing in common . . . We women pass on the human ammunition of 'only sons' to fill up the gaps, so that when the 'common soldier' looks back before 'going over the top' he may see the women of the British race at his heels, reliable, independent, uncomplaining (63)."

Sometimes war fever broke into actual violence in raids on shops whose owners had German names. The suffragette, Sylvia Pankhurst, described such an incident. "A crowd was advancing at a run, a couple of lads on bicycles leading, a swarm of children on the fringes, screaming like gulls . . . a woman was in the midst – her blouse half torn off, her fair hair fallen, her face contorted with pain and terror, blood running down her bare white arm. A big drunken man flung her to the ground. She was lost to sight . . . 'Oh, my God! Oh, they are kicking her!' a woman screamed . . . Alas, poor patriotism! What foolish cruelties are committed in thy name . . . (64)"

Britain was also a rapidly changing society by 1916. Michael Macdonagh, a close observer of London life in wartime, noted some novelties in the streets. "The drabness of civilians is very noticeable. What shabbiness in dress! . . . The cause is to be found on the walls and hoardings. Recruiting posters have been replaced by economy posters. 'Spend less! Save more!' 'Buy only war savings certificates! . . .'

"Soldiers again abound. Many in blue – convalescent from wounds, attended by nurses – are being driven in waggonettes to see the sights. Very conspicuous on the pavements are the numbers

DESIGNED BY LT GEN SIR R S S BADEN POWELL

Are <u>YOU</u> in this?

The "shirker" stands aside while everyone else toils for the war effort

of Dominion soldiers – tall, lean fellows, springy in their walk, wearing broad brimmed khaki hats, gay with feathers . . .

"Several hansoms have reappeared . . . looking as smart as ever. What seemed to me the whimsical anti-climax was the sight of two old four-wheeled cabs – the familiar growlers of Victorian times – brought out from the dark cobwebbed corners of some stable with appropriately ancient drivers (65)."

Beside the novelties, the Defence of the Realm Act (D.O.R.A.) affected all spheres of life. Censorship was imposed; taxation increased; strikes forbidden; food controlled. The grip of the state on the individual tightened.

Women at work There was new opportunity for women to work, taking the place of men in the army. The woman worker was remarkable in her many new roles. "Women are to be seen at work everywhere," wrote Macdonagh. "You see them at the wheel of motor-cars and motor drays. You see them handling the reins of horse-drawn vehicles. They are ticket collectors at underground and tube stations. At hotels and offices the lift-boy has become a lift-girl. The hall porter at some of the big hotels is an Amazon . . . But my favourite is the young 'conductorette,' on trams and buses, in her smart jacket, short skirts to the knees and leather leggings (66)."

July, 1915, had been a turning point in the movement towards women's work; Mrs. Emmeline Pankhurst, the suffragette, had led a parade of 30,000 women, to press for "The Right to Serve." Macdonagh was there. The parade "included a 'Pageant of the Allies' . . . A girl in white, carrying an armful of roses, represented England . . . There were numerous banners with inscriptions, such as 'Women's battle cry is work, work, work' and 'Shells made by women may save their husbands' lives' (67)."

"Munition-ettes" Lloyd George, then Minister of Munitions, took on thousands of women to work in the new armaments factories. The "muni-tionettes" earned good wages, but they endured dangers, too, in working with explosives. T.N.T. especially caused the skin to go yellow, making the women into "canaries." One eyewitness called them "Amazonian beings . . . bereft of all charm of appearance, clothed anyhow, skin stained a yellow-brown even to the roots of their dishevelled hair (68)." Lloyd George, praising their courage, described an explosion at a factory. "Lord Lee (my representative) ran into a busy little woman, white-faced but resolute. 'Is this where the explosion took place?' he asked. 'Yes,' she answered. She was in charge of the hut and when he entered it, he saw bloodstains on the floor, and the survivors carrying on at full speed (69)."

Two of Lloyd George's "munitionettes" and the shells for the battle
bombardment

Despite these dangers morale was high. At Woolwich Arsenal
"Thoughts for munition workers" were hung on the walls.
"Motive for work: Patriotism. A munition worker is as important as the soldier in the trenches, and on her his life depends."
Another read: "Aim: output. Anyone who limits this is a traitor
to sweethearts, husbands, and brothers fighting. One minute lost
by sixty girls means the loss of an hour's output (70)."

Nursing was the other great opportunity for women to serve. *Nursing*
Many a girl of the upper and middle classes went to serve as a
V.A.D. (Voluntary Aid Detachment). The contribution of women
to the war effort was a major factor in their winning the vote
when the war ended.

A second novelty on the Home Front was the air raid. The *Air raids*
German Zeppelins were giant dirigible airships, flying symbols
of German prestige before the war. In January, 1915, they first
raided England, bombing coastal towns in East Anglia. Soon they
were bombing London itself. A wave of amazement and anger
swept the country. As the German Press commented, it was a

37

THE ZEPPELIN RAIDS : THE VOW OF VENGEANCE
Drawn for 'The Daily Chronicle' by Frank Brangwyn ARA

'DAILY CHRONICLE' READERS ARE
COVERED AGAINST THE RISKS OF
BOMBARDMENT BY ZEPPELIN OR
AEROPLANE

"The Vow of Vengeance" by Frank Brangwyn: a soldier swears to
avenge British civilians killed by a Zeppelin attack

significant moment in British history. "German genius has at last ended the legend of England's invulnerable insularity; no longer is she protected by the sea . . . Now the first Zeppelin has appeared over England and has extended its fiery greeting to our enemy. It has come to pass that which the English have long feared and repeatedly contemplated with terror . . . the most modern air weapon, a triumph of German inventiveness and the sole possession of the German army has shown itself capable of crossing the sea and carrying the war to the soil of Old England (71)."

To the British, the "aerial ghouls" seemed yet another example of German "frightfulness." The horrors of war were no longer so remote. D. H. Lawrence described a raid: "The awful noise and excitement . . . There in the sky, like some god vision, a Zeppelin, and the searchlights catching it, so that it gleamed like a manifestation in the heavens, then losing it, so that only the strange drumming came down out of the sky where the searchlights tangled their feelers. There it was again, high, high, high, tiny, pale . . . and the crashes of the guns and the awful hoarseness of shells bursting in the city . . . (72)"

Several methods of defence and counter attack were used against the clumsy, vulnerable airship. The blackout was the most striking result of air raids. "The lights of London may be said to have been extinguished," wrote Macdonagh. "Blinds are drawn in private houses before the lights are lit . . . There are no lights on the river front or on the bridges; omnibuses and tram-cars are curtained; motorists coming to London from the country are required by military patrols on the outskirts to turn off their headlights . . . We have grown accustomed to look upwards in the dark. The night sky has been revealed to us for the first time. We have come to realize in London the beauty of the dark blue sky sparkling with the constellations (73)." *The blackout*

There were 51 raids by Zeppelins during the war causing 1,913 casualties and half a million pounds worth of damage. The material cost was slight compared to the shock of knowing that Britain was no longer protected by the sea.

Conscription was a third major shock for British life. As the flow of volunteers for the army declined, the Government *Conscription* inched towards the revolution of compulsory military service for all. The Derby scheme, a last attempt to gather volunteers, failed. Mr. Asquith, the Prime Minister, then introduced his Universal Conscription Bills in early 1915. Every fit man between 18 and 41 was to do military service unless he was exempted for special work.

Conscientious
objectors
Controversy was stirred about an exemption based on a "conscientious objection to the undertaking of combatant service." Tribunals of local officials were set up across the country to consider appeals. There was little sympathy for the "conscientious objectors." The *Daily Express* jeered, "New Name for Slackers . . . it is perfectly certain that every coward and slacker in the land will find his conscience forbids him to fight (74)." Other papers called them "pasty faces," "flimsy sentimentalists," or "anarchists." Horatio Bottomley, in a popular weekly magazine called *John Bull,* commented, "The conscientious objector is a fungus growth – a human toadstool – which should be uprooted without further delay (75)."

The objectors were, at best, men of passionate sincerity. The two objector societies were the Union of Democratic Control (U.D.C.) and the No-Conscription Fellowship (N.C.F.). They were dominated by Socialists, who believed in international workers' unity, and Quakers, whose religious principles made them pacifists. The N.C.F. manifestos set out their ideals. "We yield to no one in our admiration of the self-sacrifice, the courage and unflagging devotion of our fellow countrymen who have felt it their duty to take up arms. Nevertheless, we cannot undertake the same form of service . . . for us 'Thou shalt not kill' means what it says. The destruction of our fellow men . . . appals us; we cannot assist in the cutting off of one generation from life (76)." To support such ideals, the objectors endured a lonely strugle against persecution.

Propaganda
The last great novelty that came to wartime Britain was propaganda, a new, sinister weapon of war. The British Government had first to create hatred of Germany; the German army's conduct during the invasion of "Gallant Little Belgium" gave the propagandists great scope. It was said that the German policy of "frightfulness" had allowed violation of women, mutilation

of children, looting and destruction of valuable property. The many rumours were gathered by the Government into the Bryce Report, which consisted of "eyewitness" descriptions of sadistic cruelties, such as this episode involving a German patrol in Belgium. "The wife came out with a little sucking child. She put the child down and sprang at the Germans like a lioness. She clawed their faces. One of the Germans took a rifle and struck her a tremendous blow with the butt on the side of the head. Another took his bayonet and . . . thrust it through the child. He then put his rifle on his shoulder with the child upon it; its little arms stretched out once or twice . . . (77)" Whether true or not, these reports were effective propaganda.

The German claim to have a higher kind of civilization, a *kultur* of *Denker und Dichter* (philosophers and poets), was now sneeringly dismissed by the British. The image of the treacherous, bullying German was created. A *Daily Graphic* editorial commented typically, "Your German is a born bully, saturated with arrogance. His mind is diseased. That is the root cause of the loathing which the world has now acquired for Germany. It has been the origin of all her nameless crimes against civilization and humanity. For all its veneer of civilization, German nature is closer than any others to the elemental brutality of prehistoric days (78)." *The image of the German*

The German vices were personified in Kaiser William II and his son, "Little Willie," the Crown Prince, both easy figures to caricature. They formed a focus of hatred. The Kaiser was the arch-enemy, "the War Lord," "the mad-dog of Europe," "the Beast of the Apocalypse." The *Daily Mail* said of him, "Neither England nor civilized Europe and Asia is going to be set trembling by lunatic William, even though by his orders, Rheims Cathedral has been destroyed. This last act of the barbarian chief will only draw us all closer together to be rid of a scourge the like of which the world has never seen before. The madman is piling up the logs of his own pyre. We can have no terror of the monster; we shall clench our teeth in determination that, if we die to the last man, the modern Judas and his hell-begotten brood shall be wiped out (79)." *Kaiser William II*

Wild rumours fabricated German atrocities in the emotional, *The "corpse factory"* 41 unstable atmosphere of the war years. The best-known lie was the German "corpse factory," where corpses from the battlefields were supposedly boiled down to obtain fats. The lie had been created by reversing the captions on two photographs showing dead horses and dead men. A propaganda pamphlet was produced. "Attila's Huns were guilty of atrocious crimes, but they never desecrated the bodies of dead soldiers . . . by improvising a factory for the conversion of human corpses into fats and oils and fodder for pigs . . . It is an illustration of their much vaunted efficiency! A sign of their pious *kultur*! (80)"

Vague British war aims

The energy put into this negative propaganda against Germany disguised how thin British war aims were. The Government had no concrete objectives. So the people were told that the homeland was in danger, the ancient heritage threatened. H. G. Wells hopefully saw the confrontation as "the war to end war." Horatio Bottomley echoed him. "This is the last great upheaval of our primitive savagery, a dying demonstration of that barbarism from which we have all risen . . . When the roar of the cannon has died away and the blood has ceased flowing, the scales may drop from our eyes . . . we may . . . see before us a brighter and clearer road with the Prince of Peace at its end (81)."

Popular support for the war

There was a general, vague belief in "the rightness" of "The Cause." Families everywhere loyally supported their menfolk in the services. Sylvia Pankhurst saw "in the tiny, shell-paned windows of country cottages, cards with red crosses indicated that a member of the household was fighting at the front. On the parlour walls, among flower illuminated cards bearing scriptural texts and the faded pictures of parents and grandparents, were the photographs of soldier sons and husbands, and cheap magazine colour prints of khaki heroes . . . (82)"

Such was the atmosphere, such were the changes in Britain when the Somme Battle began.

4 Preparations for Battle

FOR BOTH SIDES in the war, 1915 was "the year of failure." All attempts to break the trench deadlock were defeated. For the British, the Battle of Neuve Chapelle, in March, was a miniature of all the great battles to follow: the artillery barrage; a mass advance of troops to seize the enemy line; a delayed second assault; a shortage of ammunition; German reinforcements rushed to seal the gap; and the machine gun finally triumphant in defence. In September came the "Big Push" at Loos in the French mining country. Tragic confusion reigned after initial success; 50,000 men were lost. *British battle failures*

No more successful was the novel British strategy of an attack on the Dardanelles in the East to open a new front. This campaign became bogged down in yet more trenches after the landings of troops at Gallipoli in Turkey. It was abandoned in December, 1915. *Gallipoli campaign*

Failure brought a change of leadership. Sir John French, Commander of the B.E.F. in France, was replaced by Sir Douglas Haig on 10th December, 1915. French's reputation had been shattered at Loos, and Haig seized his chance. It was the climax of a successful career after service in India and South Africa that had brought him rapid promotion and a reputation as "the thinking soldier."

For the soldiers of 1916, Haig was a new hope. A Kitchener volunteer described him as "a wonderful looking man, with a very firm chin and dark blue eyes . . . He is rather short but very broad and strong looking. He looks at everything so directly and deliberately . . . He never takes his eyes off the eyes of the man he is *Sir Douglas Haig*

43

talking to (83).''

Argument still rages about his work in the war. For some he was "The Master of the Field," who won the victories of 1918; for others he was "The Butcher," whose reputation is clouded by the bloody failures on the Somme and at Ypres in 1917. Lloyd George saw him as "brilliant to the top of his army boots," the typical example of the elderly general miles behind the front sending young men to death in thousands.

Haig's remoteness   His remoteness was, perhaps, his worst fault. Philip Gibbs wrote bitterly about his headquarters at Montreuil, sixty miles from the trenches, "a place where the pageantry of war still maintained its old and dead tradition . . . Often one saw the Commander-in-Chief starting for an afternoon ride, a fine figure, nobly mounted, with two A.D.C.s and an escort of lancers. A pretty sight, with fluttering pennons on all their lances and horses groomed to the last hair. It was prettier that the real thing up in the Salient [Ypres] or beyond the Somme, where dead bodies lay on upheaved earth among ruins and slaughtered trees. War at Montreuil was quite a pleasant occupation for elderly generals . . . (84)"

Haig watched his soldiers depart for battle with apparent detachment. He wrote to his wife, "I feel quite sad at times when I see them march past me, knowing as I do how many must pay the full penalty before we can have peace (85)." The soldiers, despite their loyalty to Haig, replied with a sardonic song about this kind of authority.

> *Forward, Joe Soap's army, marching without fear,*
> *With our old commander safely in the rear,*
> *He boasts and skites from morn to night*
> *And thinks he's very brave,*
> *But the men who really did the job*
> *Are dead and in their grave . . .*

In December, 1915, representatives of the Allies – Britain, France, Russia and Italy – met at Chantilly, headquarters of the French Commander-in-Chief, Maréchal Joffre. They decided that there were to be co-ordinated offensives in the summer of 1916.

Haig and Joffre met to decide the place for a Franco-British attack. Haig's favourite idea was an attack in Flanders combined with a naval landing in Belgium. Joffre favoured the area around the river Somme in Picardy because "it will be a considerable advantage to attack the enemy on a front where for long months the reciprocal activity of the troops opposed to each other has been less than elsewhere. The ground besides is in many places favourable to the development of a powerful offensive (86)." Forty French divisions and twenty-five British divisions were to attack together on a forty-mile front. *Joffre's Somme plan*

Haig, following his instruction that "closest co-operation between the French and British as a United Army must be the governing policy," reluctantly yielded to Joffre's plan. If the armies succeeded in breaking through the line, however, there were no great strategic prizes to be won. One observer commented that the place for the Battle "seems to have been arrived at solely because the British would be bound to take part in it" on that sector (87). In this ill-conceived way, the Battle was planned.

However, the Germans attacked first on the Western Front. *German plans* 4!

Erich von Falkenhayn, Chief of the General Staff of the German Army, had presented a new plan to the Kaiser. The best way to attack the arch enemy, Britain, was by defeating France, "her best sword." France should be tempted to defend to the death some vital point on the Front. "The uncertain method of a mass breakthrough . . . is unnecessary," he wrote. "Within our reach behind the French sector of the Western Front there are objectives for the retention of which the French General Staff would be compelled to throw in every man they have. If they do, the forces of France will bleed to death . . . (88)"

As a target for this policy of "attrition," Falkenhayn selected Verdun, a fortress city with a particular emotional meaning for the French. On 21st February, 1916, the heroic and brutally wasteful French defence of Verdun began. A crater zone eight miles wide was made by the twenty-three million shells poured out by both sides. In the "mincing machine," wrote a French officer, "you eat, you drink beside the dead, you sleep in the midst of the dying, you laugh and sing in the company of corpses." The fighting continued until autumn "like a gigantic forge that never stopped day or night (89)." *Battle of Verdun*

Verdun altered the proposed Somme Battle: it now had to be a relief operation and only sixteen French divisions could now be spared for it.

In the spring of 1916, Haig sent the Commander of the British Fourth Army, General Sir Henry Rawlinson, to examine the area where his men were to attack. The capture of a long ridge between the River Somme and its tributary, the Ancre, was to be the main effort of the Battle. In the wide marshy valley of the Ancre was Albert, a little red brick town notable for its large church, whose tower was capped by a gilt statue of the Virgin and Child. The tower had been shattered by shell fire and now the statue hung precariously; "that figure once stood triumphantly on the cathedral tower; now it is bowed as by the last extremity of grief (90)." Soldiers on both sides treated this landmark, "the hanging Virgin," with superstitious awe. From Albert, a Roman road went straight over the ridge to the German-held town of Bapaume, a first target for the British offensive. *The Somme battlefield*

The trench lines cut through several villages. The Germans had *The German lines* 47

Opposite The "hanging Virgin" of Albert Basilica, a famous Somme landmark

tunnelled beneath the villages and turned them into "fortresses." Their names were to acquire a sinister significance for British troops in the coming Battle. Between villages, there were "redoubts" (knots of trenches) on crests of ridges. The trenches were easy to dig. "The soil of the place is the best conceivable for digging for it cuts like cheese and hardens like brick in dry weather," wrote John Buchan, the first historian of the Somme (91).

German dugouts Under their lines, the Germans scooped huge dugouts to protect themselves from bombardment. These were a revelation when they were captured by the British, as Buchan described. "The greatest marvels were the dugouts. One at Fricourt had nine rooms and five bolt-holes: it had iron doors, gas curtains, linoleum on the floors, wallpaper and pictures on the walls, and boasted a good bathroom, electric lights and electric bells . . . Many of the dugouts had two storeys, a thirty foot staircase, beautifully furnished, leading to the first suite and a second staircase of the same length conducting to a lower storey (92)."

German advantages The Germans held the advantage along the ridge. From their chain of villages and redoubts they could inflict a murderous cross-fire from hundreds of machine-guns, if they were attacked. Two further complete trench systems lay behind the front line. The German army had fought here in 1870 and had made a special study of this ground in their military academies before the war. They had had two years to prepare their defences. The British would have to attack uphill. Winston Churchill wrote later, "The policy of the French and British commanders had selected as the point for their offensive what was undoubtedly the strongest and most perfectly defended position in the world (93)."

Such was the ground General Rawlinson surveyed. A first plan of Battle was made by the British commanders:

The battle plan The aims of the Battle: (1) to relieve pressure on Verdun; (2) to inflict loss on the enemy; (3) to make a gap in the German lines, to restore open warfare and cause a German retreat.

Methods of attack: (1) A five day initial bombardment would smash German trenches and strongholds. (2) On "Z" day, 29th June, men of The Fourth Army, advancing in "wave formation" would occupy the first and eventually the second German trench system from Serre to Maricourt, a fourteen mile Front. The French Sixth Army would advance further south. (3) The Reserve Army under General Gough, with three cavalry divisions, would pass through the gap to take Bapaume. (4) The infantry would then move north "rolling up" the German trenches towards Arras. The cavalry would advance on Cambrai and Douai. Thus the German front might collapse. (5) The Third Army was to attack Gommecourt on "Z" day to provide a diversion of enemy fire. (6) If the Somme Thrust was held up, "the most profitable course will probably be to transfer our main efforts rapidly to another position of the British front."

Liddell-Hart commented on the weaknesses of this plan. *Weaknesses* "In outline, the plan was shrewdly designed, and Haig was wise *of the plan* to take such long views. But he does not seem to have looked clearly enough at the ground beneath his feet. The very belief in such far reaching possibilities suggests a failure to diagnose the actual conditions. There was a fundamental unrealism in a plan which, while discarding the old and ever-new master key of surprise, made no pretence to provide a substitute (94)."

Detailed preparations began: new railways and roads were *Preparations* constructed; 120 miles of water pipes laid; tented accommodation for half a million men and 100,000 horses was brought in; miles of telephone cables were given a "six foot bury." Mines were tunnelled and charged under enemy strongpoints; barbed wire cages for prisoners built; casualty clearing stations and huge mass graves, "as big as half a football pitch," prepared. The guns promised by Lloyd George that should stand "wheel to wheel," were placed on their sites.

Overhead, aeroplanes shot down the German "sausage" *Air activity* observation balloons. "In the past few days," wrote a German soldier in a letter, "the air has been alive with aviators . . . Their airmen are attacking our captive balloons, too, which is the same thing as putting our eyes out. Meanwhile the sky is black with enemy balloons (95)." Allied air superiority over the Somme was to last until October. The enemy lines were constantly photographed and their supply routes bombed.

Thousands of men converged on Picardy during June, 1916, in *March to the* an atmosphere charged with drama. To some it was a relief to *Somme* 49

The road to the Somme: thousands of soldiers marched through Picardy in June, 1916

be out of the trenches moving through the summer countryside, as Wyn Griffith, a junior officer, remembered. "We walked with a swing, we sang on the march; men began to laugh, to argue, and even to quarrel, a sure sign of recovery from the torpor of winter. We were going into a battle . . . from which few of us could hope to return, but at the moment we were many miles from war, and the hedges were rich with dogrose and honey-suckle (96)."

Some, like David Jones, the poet, liked the new sort of countryside the troops marched through. The low hills of Picardy were a change after the flatness of Flanders. "The south road gleamed scorching white its wide plotted curve; you couldn't see the turned tail of the column, for the hot dust, by ten o'clock . . . Reveille was at 4.30 again next day; there was chalk beneath the turf where they lay at the third fallout; and once they halted to let pass at a crossroads a Regiment of another Division . . . they drew to the right of the road for tractored howitzers, their camouflage paint blistering at noonday; you could see the cared for moving parts, glistening from under, in deep shadow, the thrown tar-paulin, heavy on the outside with white deposit; a lorry with aeroplane parts, and more artillery – for the magnetic south (97)."

Yet others were full of tension and fear about the ordeal of battle. Henry Williamson reconstructed his thoughts in his novel, *The Golden Virgin*. "The wind waves of young summer were upon the barleys, the wheat was upright and rustling, the oats shook their green sprays. Old men with scythes were cutting hay to the tramp-tramp-tramp of nailed boots between the ever widening rows of poplars shaking all their leaves like little heliographs or as though waving goodbye. They marched through villages of white washed pise and thatch, where children stood and stared, but waved no more; for hundreds and thousands of *les Anglais* had already passed that way, singing, whistling and shouting the same remarks.

"In the heat they rested on the grasses along the verges of the road, under the poplars with their ceaseless flashing leaves ... No, he must not put his feelings into leaves, as though he were of leaves crying to the wind, strew me not dead upon mother Earth, nor these poor men with me, brown withered leaves upon the earth, lost to the sun . . . (98)"

Just before the Battle, General Rawlinson reviewed the preparations: he had eighteen divisions of infantry, containing 519,324 men. Sixty percent of the attacking force was to be New Army men. He had over 1,500 guns, one to every 57 yards of front. There was no shortage of ammunition.

In the battle zone, most movements were made by night. Cecil Lewis, the R.F.C. pilot, was struck by the bustling activity. "By day the roads were deserted; but as soon as dark fell, they were thick with transport, guns, ammunition - trains and troops, all moving up through Albert . . . we used to lean over the mess windowsill and watch them, dim and fantastic silhouettes, passing in the flicker of oil lamps . . . the noisy nightmare gave us the illusion of victory . . . the sinister ghosts hailed us as they passed, and we shouted back to them catch phrases of the time, ribald greetings, sardonic cheers . . . Endlessly, night after night, it went on . . . Yet, when dawn came, all signs of it were gone. There was the deserted road, the tumbledown farm house, the serene and silent summer morning (99)."

Soon it became obvious to the Germans of General Von

Overleaf The massive, but ineffective, seven-day bombardment on the Somme in June, 1916

Below's Second Army on the Somme front that an attack was coming. Agents in Britain confirmed these fears. A member of the British Government, in a speech to munition workers, explained the postponement of Whitsun holidays. "How inquisitive we are! It should suffice that we ask for a postponement of the holidays and to the end of July. This fact should speak volumes." Crown Prince Rupprecht noted in his diary, "It certainly does so speak. It contains the surest proof that there will be a great British offensive before long (100)." The German defences on the Somme were strengthened, though Falkenhayn was convinced the real attack would come further north.

Training for Battle

In the days before battle, some attempt was made to provide training. Rehearsals were carried out on land behind the lines with trenches marked out by tapes. All along the front on "Z" day, troops were to advance "at a steady pace" in wave formation, each man five yards from his neighbour, each line a hundred yards ahead of the next. A pamphlet, "Fourth Army Tactical Notes" promised success. "A single line of men has usually failed; two lines have generally failed, but sometimes succeeded; three lines have generally succeeded, but sometimes failed, and four lines have generally succeeded." These lines of men were to present perfect targets for machine guns in the first attack.

However, High Command allowed no argument. The pamphlet continued: "Men must learn to obey by instinct, without thinking, so that in times of stress, they will act as they are accustomed to do . . . Finally it must be remembered that all criticism by subordinates of their superiors and of orders received . . . will in the end recoil on the heads of the critics and undermine their authority with those below them . . ." The pamphlet concluded grandly: "All must be prepared for heavy casualties . . . The magnitude of the interest at stake necessitates the greatest self sacrifice from one and all (101)." This advice, at least, the soldiers of the Somme were to follow.

Preliminary bombardment

On 24th June, the mighty collection of artillery began the preliminary bombardment. A hurricane of fire fell on the German lines day and night for the following week. In all, one and half million shells were fired, at a cost of some six million pounds.

The grandeur of the spectacle impressed all observers. "My

Lord the gun has come into his own, and his kingdom today is large – it is the world," wrote Adrian Stephen, an artillery observer (102). Another officer described the dramatic display at night. "Carroll and I stood on top of one of our gun pits one pitch dark night, watching the show . . . Speech was, of course, impossible, and one could only stand and feel the thousands of tons of metal rushing away from one . . . (103)"

Even in England, the guns could be heard. "They had never spoken before with so huge a voice," wrote Edmund Blunden, "their sound crossed the sea. In Southdown villages, the school children sat wondering at the incessant drumming and the rattling of the windows . . . (104)" The vibrations could even be *felt*, according to Vera Brittain, a London nurse. "We already knew that a tremendous bombardment had begun, for we could feel the vibration of the guns at Camberwell (105)."

The Germans endured the onslaught in their deep dugouts. Damage was not as great as intended. Some of the poorly-made ammunition failed to explode, leaving the ground littered with duds. The wire was uncut in many places. German casualties were not heavy; British raiding parties, testing the German lines, found their probes quickly repulsed.

On 27th and 28th June, heavy rain fell, delaying the assault of "Z" day until Saturday, 1st July. In muddy trenches, men prepared themselves for the ordeal. In letters of farewell to families at home, young officers express the noble and poignant voice of "The Lost Generation." A lieutenant wrote: "The day has almost dawned when I shall really do my little bit in the cause of civilization. Tomorrow morning, I shall take my men . . . over the top to do our bit in the first attack . . . Should it be God's holy will to call me away, I am quite prepared to go . . . I could not wish for a finer death, and you, dear Mother and Dad, will know that I died doing my duty to my God, my country and my King (106)."

Last letters

Another wrote, "The prospect of pain naturally appals me somewhat, and I am taking morphia with me into battle . . . Our cause is a good one and I believe that I am doing right in fighting (107)."

A third wrote, "I have been looking at the stars and thinking

about what an immense distance they are away. What an insignificant thing the loss of say 40 years of life is compared to them . . . Well, Goodbye, you darlings . . . This letter is going to be posted if – (108)"

Attacking battalions were addressed by senior officers in grossly over-optimistic terms. "You will find the Germans all dead; not even a rat will have survived." They had merely to walk across No Man's land and occupy the German trenches. A general, speaking to the Royal Fusiliers, said, "You are probably aware that we are now taking part in the greatest battle ever fought by British troops . . . of far more importance than any fight since Waterloo . . . You are fighting for your country, and . . . for Christianity and Humanity. You are fighting for truth and justice against oppression. We are fighting for liberty against slavery (109)."

Most men were to carry at least 60 to 70 pounds in weight, *Heavy battle* which, said the Official History, "made it difficult to get out of a *equipment* trench, impossible to move much quicker than a slow walk, or to rise and lie down quickly (110)." For men in rear waves, there were bulkier burdens: barbed-wire reels, duckboards, even carrier pigeons in baskets. "In a field close by," noted Philip Gibbs, "some troops were being ticketed with yellow labels fastened to their backs. It was to distinguish them so that artillery observers might know them from the enemy . . . Something in the sight of those yellow tickets made me feel sick (111)." Others carried tin mirrors on their backs to catch the eye of aeroplane observers.

On the evening of 30th June, Geoffrey Malins, sent to film *Eve of Battle* the Battle by the Government, watched the soldiers relaxing. "It was not long before little red fires were gleaming out of the dugout entrances, and crowds of men were crouching round, heating up their canteens of water, some frying pieces of meat, others heating soup, and all the time laughing and carrying on a most animated conversation. From other groups came the subdued humming of favourite songs . . . And these men knew that they were going 'over the top' in the morning . . . they knew that many would not be alive tomorrow night, yet I never saw a sad face, nor heard a word of complaint . . . (112)"

Opposite A last letter home: a young officer writes from the trenches before going into battle

The eve of battle: assault troops enjoy a last meal on 30th June, 1916.
A still from the Somme film

An officer left in reserve watched men pass to the front line. "Now, for the first time, there is an 'eve of battle' feeling in the air. One began to wonder what Great Uncle Joseph felt like before the Battle of Waterloo . . . (113)"

Last thoughts Zero hour was 7.30 next morning. Sir Douglas Haig, encouraged by the initial success of the Russian Brussilov offensive early in June, was confident. He wrote to his wife, "You must know that I feel that every step in my plan has been taken with the Divine Help (114)." In his diary, disregarding several protests about uncut wire, he noted, "the weather is favourable for tomorrow. With God's help, I feel hopeful. The men are in splendid spirits . . . The wire has never been so well cut nor the artillery preparation so thorough (115)."

Back in London, the hospitals were ready to receive the expected casualties. Nurse Vera Brittain described "the sickening apprehension of those days . . . Hour after hour . . . we added to the long rows of waiting beds, so sinister in their white expectant emptiness (116)."

Before going into battle, a young officer, W. N. Hodgson, had written a farewell poem which ended (117):

> *I, that on my familiar hill*
> *Saw with uncomprehending eyes*
> *A hundred of Thy sunsets spill*
> *Their fresh and sanguine sacrifice,*
> *Ere the sun swing's his noonday sword*
> *Must say goodbye to all of this!*
> *By all delights that I shall miss,*
> *Help me to die, O Lord.*

He was to die next day, with 21,000 other British soldiers in the bloodiest disaster in British military history.

5 The Blackest Day: 1st July, 1916

DAWN CAME UP, grey and misty at 4 a.m. The sky was to clear *Dawn* to give a hot day of radiant blue sky, that was to be such a contrast with the slaughter on the battlefield. Henry Williamson remained haunted by this, "July the first, that dream-like day of terror and great heat . . . that brazen sunny morning which appeared with voiceless glassy pain in his mind at odd moments of the day and night (118)."

Brigadier Crozier remembered the atmosphere of that night and dawn as he waited below Thiepval. "Sleep does not come. I wander about among the men, who are all lying on the ground, their arms piled, their equipment ready. Most are asleep. I talk to some in lowered tones who are not already asleep, looking at the stars in contemplation . . . Dawn breaks. The birds begin to sing . . . (119)"

At 6.25, the temporary silence was shattered by the final intensive bombardment of the German lines. Cecil Lewis, already flying, watched from above. "We climbed away on that cloudless summer morning towards the lines. There was a soft white haze over the ground that the summer's heat would quickly disperse . . . The devastating effect of the week's bombardment could be seen. Square miles of country had been ripped and blasted to a pock-marked desolation . . . Now the hurricane bombardment started. Half an hour to go! The whole salient from Beaumont-Hamel down to the marshes of the Somme covered to a depth of several hundred yards with a coverlet of white wool-smoking shell bursts! It was the greatest bombardment of the war, the greatest in the history of the world (120)."

Opposite "Over the top": British troops go into action on 1st July, 1916. Two stills from the Somme film

For the men beneath, waiting to leap from their trenches, it seemed an omen of success. "It was wonderful music – the mightiest I have ever heard. It seemed to throb, throb into our very veins . . . And then, at last, ten minutes before zero, the guns opened their lungs. The climax had been reached. One felt inclined to laugh with the fierce exhilaration of war. After all, it was our voice, the voice of a whole Empire at war (121)."

To a New Army N.C.O., R. H. Tawney, "it seemed as though the air were . . . vibrating with the solemn pulses of enormous wings . . . yet all the time one was intent on practical details, wiping the trench dirt off the bolt of one's rifle, reminding the men of what each was to do, and when the message came round 'five minutes to go,' seeing that all bayonets were fixed (122)."

Waiting
soldiers
The poet John Masefield recorded some last thoughts of men about to "Go over the top." "I thought of all the people that I liked, and things I wanted to do, and told myself that that was all over, that I had done with that; but I was sick with sorrow all the same . . . There was a terrific noise and confusion, but I kept thinking that I heard a lark . . . A rat dodged down the trench among the men, and the men hit at it, but it got away . . . Then I thought again: 'in about five minutes from now I shall be dead.' I envied people whom I had seen in billets two nights before. I thought, 'They will be alive at dinner time today, and tonight they'll be snug in bed; but where shall I be? My body will be out there in No-Man's land . . . What is done to people when they die? (123)"

Just before zero the great mines under the German strongpoints were exploded. At Hawthorn Ridge, near Beaumont-Hamel, Geoffrey Malins filmed the explosion. "Then it happened. The ground where I stood gave a mighty convulsion . . . Then, for all the world like a gigantic sponge, the earth rose into the air to the height of hundreds of feet. Higher and higher it rose, and with a horrible grinding roar the earth fell back upon itself (124)."

Above La Boiselle, Cecil Lewis saw the mines beside "The Road" (between Albert and Bapaume) blown up. "The earthy column rose . . . like the silhouette of some great cypress tree . . . a moment later came the second mine . . . Then dust cleared and we saw the two white eyes of the craters (125)." These explosions were omens of the violence that the Battle was now to unleash; their craters, too big to fill in, remain today as the last scars on the battlefield.

Shortly afterwards, at 7.30, 60,000 British soldiers, on a front of fourteen miles, climbed their trench ladders to advance on the German lines. John Masefield wrote later, "All along that Old Front Line of the English, there came a whistling and a crying. The men of the first wave climbed up the parapets, in tumult, darkness and the presence of death, and, having done with all pleasant things, advanced across No-Man's land to begin the Battle of the Somme (126)." *Zero hour*

For individuals, zero hour was a relief. This was the soldier's personal test of courage. R. H. Tawney noted his feelings. "At 7.30, we went up the ladders, doubled through the gaps in the wire, and lay down, waiting for the line to form up on each side of us. When it was ready, we went forward . . . There was a bright light in the air and the tufts of coarse grass were grey with dew . . . I had been worried by the thought: 'Suppose one should lose one's head and get other men cut up! Suppose one's legs should take fright and refuse to move!' Now I knew it was all right . . . I felt quite happy and self possessed (127)."

In front of La Boiselle an officer remembered, "I started off like many another officer with a cigarette well alight. Many of the men were puffing at their pipes. Officers and men exchanged 'good-lucks,' 'cheerohs,' and other expressions of comradeship and encouragement (128)." Others began with bravado – to the sound of a hunting horn, to the skirl of pipes, or, near Montauban, behind a football kicked at the German lines. Irish Protestant soldiers went into action beside Thiepval wearing their Orange Order sashes and badges. *The advance*

Observers behind could see little. Near Fricourt, Siegfried Sassoon wrote in his diary, "The sunlight flashes on bayonets as the tiny figures move quietly forward and disappear behind mounds of trench debris . . . I am staring at a sunlit picture of Hell, and still the breeze shakes the yellow weeds and the poppies glow (129)." At Gommecourt, Charles Carrington was in reserve. "We had glimpses of a few men of the London

63

"The Surreys Play the Game": a picture from the *Illustrated London News* showing Captain Neville's men kicking a football ahead of them as they attack

Scottish in their hodden grey kilts running forward into the smoke. That was all. That and a growing hullabaloo of noise . . . You could hear the battle but you couldn't see it (130)."

The German defence The Germans emerged from their underground shelters with their machine guns when the artillery "lifted" to rear lines at 7.30. A German soldier near Ovillers recalled this rush to defence. "The machine-guns were pulled out of the dugouts and hurriedly placed in position . . . a series of extended lines of British infantry were seen moving forward from the British trenches . . . They came on at a steady pace as if expecting to find nothing alive in our front trenches . . . The rattle of machine-gun and rifle fire broke out from along the whole line of craters . . . Red rockets sped up into the blue sky as a signal to the artillery, and immediately afterwards a mass of shells from the German batteries in the rear tore through the air and burst among the advancing lines. Whole sections seemed to fall . . . All along the line, men could be seen throwing their arms into the air and collapsing never to move again . . . the noise of battle became indescribable . . . Again and again, the extended lines of British infantry broke against the

German defence like waves against a cliff, only to be beaten back
. . . (131)"

Henry Williamson, one of these attackers, advanced with his men against "the murderous rattle of German machine-guns . . . In the flame and rolling smoke I see men arising and walking forward; and I go forward with them, in a glassy delirium wherein some men seem to pause with bowed heads, and sink carefully to their knees, and roll slowly over, and lie still. Others roll and roll, and scream and grip my legs in uttermost fear, and I have to struggle to break away, while the dust and earth on my tunic changes from grey to red (132)." *The British mown down*

In the northern half of the field, advance became almost impossible against uncut enemy wire. As troops crowded desperately through the gaps, they were shot down or tangled in the barbs, "riddled with bullets like crows on a dyke." German artillery pounded No-Man's land, the explosions "like a thick belt of poplar trees." Michael Macdonagh, *The Times* correspondent, reported the experiences of Irish troops. "The men went on steadily . . . shaken only by one terror . . . that of seeing comrades of their own falling bereft of life, as in a flash, by a bullet through the brain or heart; or worse still, just as suddenly disappearing into bloody fragments amid the roar and smoke of a bursting shell. Now and then men stopped awhile trembling at the sight and aghast and . . . put their right hands over their faces as a protection to their eyes – an appeal . . . that they might be mercifully spared their sight – or else made a sweeping gesture of the arm as if to brush aside the bullets which buzzed about them like venomous insects (133)."

Brigadier Crozier could see the casualties piling up in front of Thiepval, "rows upon rows of British soldiers lying dead, dying or wounded in No Man's land. Here and there I see an officer urging on his followers. Occasionally I can see the hands thrown up and then a body flops to the ground . . . I look south-ward from a different angle and see heaped up masses of British corpses suspended on the German wire in front of Thiepval strong-hold, while live men rush forward in orderly procession to swell the weight of numbers in the spider's web (134)." *Success in*

Almost everywhere on and north of "the Road" (between *the South* 65

Albert and Bapaume), the attackers were "like human cornstalks falling before the reaper." To the south, where No-Man's land was narrower, the attack was more successful: Fricourt was surrounded, and surrendered on 2nd July; Mametz and Montauban captured. R. H. Tawney described the advance in that sector. "We crossed three lines that had once been trenches, and tumbled into the fourth, our final objective. 'If it's all like this, it's a cake walk,' said a little man beside me, the kindest and bravest of friends . . . but he's dead . . . Far away, a thousand yards or so half left we could see kilted figures running and leaping in front of a dazzling white stonehenge, mannikins moving jerkily on a bright green cloth. 'The Jocks bombing them out of Mametz,' said someone. Then there was a sudden silence, and when I looked round I saw the men staring stupidly, like calves smelling blood, at two figures. One was doubled up over his stomach, hugging himself and frowning. The other was holding his hand out and looking at it with a puzzled expression. It was covered with blood – the fingers, I fancy, were blown off – and he seemed to be saying: 'Well, this is a funny kind of thing to have for a hand' (135)."

Confusion and rumour   Once the attack had begun, the commanders could do little – without radio, they had to rely on fragile telephone lines for communication, which were hopelessly inefficient. By midday the many rumours, mostly optimistic, had been modified by ominous facts: the corpses seen clearly in No Man's land and the lack of prisoners. But the attacks were pressed all day, amid growing confusion. Only at Montauban was there a real taste of victory, where the British troops could look east over green country. Here were enemy dead to contemplate. "They looked monstrous, lying there crumpled up, amidst a foul litter of clothes, stick bombs, old boots and bottles . . . Victory! . . . others might have been old or young. One could not tell because they had no faces and were just masses of raw flesh in uniforms . . . (136)"

French success   Further south, the French attacking with only five divisions had swept to all their objectives. Yet in the southern sector, where a breakthrough had come, no advance was made. The troops were told to dig in.

66   *Afternoon*   The afternoon dragged miserably for the wounded or survivors

trapped in No Man's land. By now R. H. Tawney was one of these. "It was very hot . . . I drank the rest of my water at a gulp. How I longed for the evening! I'd lost my watch, so I tried to tell the time by the sun . . . It stood straight overhead in an enormous arch of blue. After an age, I looked again. It still stood in the same place . . . (137)"

As evening fell on that "day of an intense blue summer beauty, full of roaring violence, and confusion of death, agony and triumph," Adrian Stephen pondered the scene (138). "Bunches of brown figures, lines of brown figures stretched out on the dried grass between the lines! Stray shrapnel shells burst among them, but they did not move. They lay still where they had fallen, or drooped motionless across the wire, not far, poor fellows, on the road to Germany (139)."

Dusk gave a chance for stretcher bearers to rescue the wounded, whose haunting cries – "as if huge wet fingers were being dragged across an enormous glass pane, rising and falling, interminable and unbearable" – chilled the minds of onlookers (140). The casualty clearing stations were now full of dreadful activity, as Philip Gibbs saw. "These were the victims of 'victory' and the red fruit of war's harvest fields . . . most of them were unconscious, breathing with the hard snuffle of dying men. Their skins were already darkening, to the death tint, which is not white. They were all plastered with grey clay, and this mud on their faces was, in some cases, mixed with thick clots of blood, making a hard encrustation from scalp to chin . . . No sound came from most of these bundles under the blankets, but from one came a long, agonizing wail, the cry of an animal in torture . . . (141)"

Evening: the wounded

It took time to appreciate the extent of the disaster. General Rawlinson, who had been given a casualty list of only 16,000, wrote that night, "I do not consider the percentage of losses is excessive." Only in the 1920s was it finally calculated that 57,470 men, half the attacking forces of the day, were killed, wounded or captured. 30,000 had been lost in the first hour. German losses were some 8,000 men, but their sufferings were to come.

Casualties

The bitterest blow fell on the New Armies. Kitchener's First Army, two years in the making, was destroyed in twelve hours;

30,419 of the volunteers were casualties.

The causes of the disaster lay in over-confidence. Too much faith had been placed in the artillery barrage. Guns concentrated on strongpoints would have been more effective. The tactics, based on the clumsy "waves formation" of troops, were equally to blame. Brigadier E. L. Spears, Liaison officer with the French, had watched attacks by both armies. "A joint attack by French and British had been ordered. At the appointed time they sprang forward . . . [the French, in] tiny groups, taking every advantage of cover, swarmed forward, intangible as will o'the wisps, illusive as quicksilver. The German artillery was baffled and their defences overrun by the handfuls of men . . . On their left, long lines of British infantry, at a few yards interval, and in perfect order, were slowly advancing . . . and they provided magnificent targets . . . The British were soon enveloped in clouds of bursting shells . . . When the thick clouds of smoke were dispelled and the greatly thinned lines were once more revealed, they were seen to be far fewer . . . How enraging to think of the irreparable waste. I remember a French artillery observation officer saying to me – 'I thought of the Crimea today,' and of what another French officer said then of the English [during the Charge of the Light Brigade]. *'C'est magnifique, mais ce n'est pas la guerre* (142)."

The over ambitious first thrust on the Somme ended in bloody catastrophe; the responsibility for this must rest squarely on the heads of the generals who conceived the unimaginative plan.

For the Press at home, the Battle was a tremendous new "story," hailed with exhilaration as "Britain's day"; "the Big Push"; "a great beginning"; "with France shoulder to shoulder, a turning point in the war (143)." The official communiqués, themselves inaccurate, were spun out to make a paper "victory." *The Observer* commented, "A grandeur of being beyond all that our country has known before is purchased for those who live by those who die. For Britain these days are only at the beginning of what may come. The New Armies, fighting with a valour and fibre never surpassed by any people, have excelled our best hopes (144)."

WELL DONE, THE NEW ARMY!

"Well Done, the New Army": a *Punch* cartoon which shows how the British Press over-estimated the gains and under-estimated the suffering of 1st July, 1916

Reality was disguised. The *Daily Graphic* said, "The toll of blood today has been fairly heavy but . . . happily there is a large proportion of slightly wounded cases, and I have seen many gallant lads with arms slung up or bandages about their heads, shouting that they are not downhearted (145)." Even Philip Gibbs was guilty of distortion. "And so, after the first day of battle, we may say, 'It is, on balance, a good day for England and

SUNDAY MORNING SPECIAL

NEWS OF THE WORLD.

No. 3,793.   [Estab. 1843.]   Telephones: 6150 Holborn   SUNDAY, JULY 2, 1916.   Telegrams: Worldly, Fleet, London.   ONE PENNY.

CERTIFIED NET SALES EXCEED TWO MILLION COPIES PER ISSUE.

The "Somme Punch" cartoon from *News of the World,* 2nd July, 1916.
The British army punches the Kaiser's nose

France' (146)." Beach-Thomas, of the *Daily Mail,* wrote in similar vein, "It will always remain a day of days in our history: Waterloo is an episode compared with it . . . The very attitudes of the dead, fallen eagerly forward, have a look of expectant hope. You would say that they died with the light of victory in their eyes (147)."

"Interviews" with wounded soldiers were popular: the most ludicrous of these were reported by A. J. Dawson. "What's the push like? . . . It's all the struggles of life crowded into an hour; it's the assertion of the bed-rock decency and goodness of our people . . . it's the future of humanity, countless millions, all the laughing little kiddies, and the slim, straight young girls and the sweet women, and the men that are to come; it's all humanity we're fighting for; whether life's to be clean and decent, free and worth having – or a Boche [German] nightmare . . . It's Hell and Heaven, and the devil and the world; and thank goodness, we're on the side of the angels – decency, not material gain – and we're going to win (148)."

Certain incidents caught Press notice: the chained German machine-gunner found near Fricourt; the whips found in dug-outs, supposedly used for driving Germans into battle; Captain Nevill's football, kicked ahead by his troops at Montauban. A *Daily Mail* poem ran (149):

> *On through the hail of slaughter*
> *Where gallant comrades fall,*
> *Where blood is poured like water,*
> *They drive the trickling ball.*
> *The fear of death before them*
> *Is but an empty name:*
> *True to the land that bore them*
> *The Surreys play the game.*

Amid this patriotic chorus, the *Manchester Guardian* struck a more sober note. "It is well not to carry satisfaction to the point of too great expectation. We are fighting a strong, determined and resourceful foe . . . It would be very unwise to underrate his powers of resistance particularly in the face of a highly menacing position. Great events may follow. But let us wait for these before clearing our throats preparatory to shouting (150)."

Wounded soldiers were tangible evidence of the Battle. Crowds gathered to watch the hospital trains pass, and hung about the great stations, like Charing Cross, to catch a glimpse of the mud-stained heroes. "At Charing Cross where there is always an amazing mixed and vital crowd, the London greeting was especially cordial . . . and you saw women buying up the street-sellers' roses and tossing them into taxis that brought the slightly wounded away . . . (151)" *The wounded arrive in London*

War maps became popular. "A sign of the quickened interest is the crowds round the map shops where the battle front is marked across Europe by a procession of Allied flags. These flags have been in the old positions so many weary months that all the pavement goers had ceased to glance at them, but now people gather and stare at the line with the hope . . . that the little flags will march on before long (152)." *War maps*

But the rhetoric of the Press could not conceal for long the real effects of the Battle. The grey spreading columns of casualties in the Press, the whole streets with drawn blinds in

71

some towns, the pathetic street shrines to the dead in London's East End told the true facts. The Somme was to bring the shadow of sudden death to every corner of the land. The curt words of the official telegram were death's messenger. The social historian, Mrs. C. S. Peel, described its effect on another woman. "The poor woman's face went white. Her cards fell out of her shaking hands . . . It was the telegram . . . her son had been killed (153)."

6 "The Battering Ram": July and August on the Somme

DESPITE THE LOSSES of 1st July, orders were issued that the attack should continue south of "the Road." The commanders' aim was to win favourable ground for an assault on the German second line that crowned the ridge. This meant the capture of several fortress villages and large woods, already rapidly filling up with German reserves.

Falkenhayn, Chief of the German General Staff, was angry at the loss of ground. "The first principle of position warfare must be to yield not one foot of ground; if it be lost, to retake it immediately by counter attack, even to the last man (154)." This stubbornness was the basis of the ugly attrition warfare that followed, as the Allied soldiers inched forward.

New British troops coming into the line on 2nd July saw sinister reminders of the previous day. George Coppard observed "hundreds of dead . . . strung out like wreckage washed up to a high water mark. Quite as many died on the enemy wire as on the ground, like fish caught in a net. They hung there in grotesque postures. Some looked as though they were praying; they had died on their knees and the wire had prevented their fall (155)." *The dead of 1st July*

Graham Greenwell, a regular officer, wrote home about the cause of this carnage. "They [the Germans] have plenty of machine-guns, which . . . can hold up armies. You would despair of ever making a big advance, especially with cavalry, if you could see the way in which troops are mown down by these little devils (156)."

Later, unfortunate men were given the ugly task of clearing away the decaying bodies. "Hundreds of them . . . were being *Clearing away the dead* 73

Opposite Crowds greeting wounded men from the Somme with flowers at Charing Cross Station in London. The Battle caused a great upsurge of feeling among people "at home"

British troops, some wearing German helmets, celebrate the fall of La Boiselle on 7th July, 1916

brought up every night on a trench railway from the front line and bundled out onto the ground," remembered Gerald Brennan, a junior officer. "Legs had broken off from trunks, heads came off at a touch and rolled away, and horrible liquids oozed out of the cavities. A sickening stench filled the air and obscene flies crept and buzzed about, not to speak of the worms that wriggled in the putrefaction . . . (157)"

British troops could now explore the captured trenches, and see, like Siegfried Sassoon near Mametz, the tragic cost of their capture. "I saw arranged by the roadside about fifty of the British dead . . . their fingers mingled in bloodstained bunches as though acknowledging the companionship of death. There was much battle gear lying about and some dead horses. There were rags and shreds of clothing, boots riddled and torn, and, when we came to the old German front-line, a sour pervasive stench, which differed from anything my nostrils had known before (158)."

Mametz wood Fighting in the first half of July yielded two major prizes:

La Boiselle, which surrendered on 6th July, and Mametz Wood, that "menacing wall of gloom," which blocked the advance until 13th July. Wyn Griffith, a junior officer, experienced the nightmare of fighting within its dense undergrowth. There were "limbs and mutilated trunks, here and there a detached head, forming splashes of red against the green leaves, and, as in advertisement of the horror of our way of life and death, and of our crucifixion of youth, one tree held in its branches a leg, with its torn flesh hanging down over a spray of leaf (159)."

By 13th July, Rawlinson considered he was ready for an assault on the German second line. He planned a daring experiment: his troops should attack in darkness after a short bombardment. He would use surprise, "this master key of all the great captains of history [which] had been rusting since the spring of 1915 (160)." His men would seize the enemy lines between Bazentin-le-petit village and Delville Wood.

At 3.20 a.m., on 14th July, the bombardment lifted and 22,000 *The night* British soldiers moved quickly to their objectives. By 10.00, a *attack* 6,000 yard gap had been made in the German trench system. Green country lay ahead. In the afternoon the cavalry picked their way forward over the old battlefield to charge High Wood, that crested the ridge. They arrived too late. The Indian horsemen with their lances were a glamorous sight as they rode down the German outposts, but they failed to capture the Wood. It would not fall to the British for two long months.

A grim war of attrition smouldered on along this battle front *Delville Wood* throughout July and August. It was too narrow to advance safely. In the centre High Wood remained, "like a dark cloud on the skyline," defying all Allied attacks. On the right, South Africans troops were sent in to capture and hold Delville Wood. German bombardment set the Wood alight, its trees blazing like torches in heavy rainstorms. The Wood became "just a collection of stakes stuck upright in the ground, looking like the broken teeth of some vicious beast (161)." Two and a half thousand South Africans died holding Delville Wood. Philip Gibbs saw the horror of the place later. "Those slashed trees, those naked trenches, those sucking shell-holes, and all the charred timber that lies about, the blood-stained bundles that once held life, build up a nightmare that men will dream again (162)." Beyond the wood, Guillemont village, "a shambles of blended horror and mystery," repulsed all assaults throughout August.

On the left flank, the village of Thiepval cramped the advance. The Allied troops could not surround it until they captured Ovillers and Pozières. On 16th July, Ovillers, "an underground city with its 2,000 men in caverns, with their electric dynamos and food stores," at last yielded (163). Australian troops were ordered to capture Pozières. North of the village lay a large ruin, Moquet Farm, honey-combed with underground passages. After bitter fighting, Pozières became, "nothing but a churned mass of debris with bricks, stones and girders and bodies pounded to nothing. There are not even tree trunks left, not a leaf, not a twig, all is buried and churned up again and buried again (164)."

The policy of "piecemeal attack" required the Australians to keep advancing towards Moquet Farm. The Australian Official Historian, C. E. W. Bean, was angry about these methods "of applying a battering-ram ten or fifteen times against the same part of the enemy's battle front with the intention of penetrating for a mile . . . into the midst of his organized defences." It was "murder," with men wasted because of "the incompetence, callousness and personal vanity of those high in authority (165)."

Bean quotes from soldiers' letters to support his protest. One described the landscape as "just one wilderness of friable [easily crumbled] grey craters so shredded and dry that it looked like an ancient ash heap in which hens have been scratching for years (166)." The bleak, lunar-like plateau towards Moquet Farm was "so gouged and blasted that the shell holes run into each other like sloughing sores." A line soldier described the troops' wretched condition. "We are lousy, stinking, ragged, unshaven, sleepless . . . My tunic is rotten with other men's blood and partly spattered with a comrade's brains (167)."

During August the countryside behind the lines resembled "a huge scattered fair or new found mining field in which, after dark, hundreds of camp fires twinkled in every direction (168)." "Happy Valley," between Fricourt and Bazentin, was the ante-

South African troops attempt to dig in during their gallant defence of
shattered Delville Wood, July, 1916

chamber to the Battle, where artillery was concentrated. "Happy
Valley was a desert," wrote the journalist, H. M. Tomlinson.
"Its surface was pulverized by myriads of feet, hooves and
wheels . . . The broad valley crawled with humans, cattle and
machinery . . . The flies darkened the food, shimmered over the
ordure, and swarmed on the clotted life in the hospital tents.

"The land around was terraced with massed batteries and
howitzers. Their crews laboured at the ranks of glistening steel
barrels, stripped to the waist. They fed them glumly and methodi-
cally . . . The machinery had been set going and the men were
its slaves . . . Work did not finish at sunset . . . Darkness was an
intermittent day; it was tremulous with an incessant glaring and
glittering . . . It was the Battle of the Somme. Giant automata
hammered ponderously on the old horizon, breaking it up. The
earth sparked and flashed under their poundings (169)."

Men shaken by savage battle action could recover in the
summer countryside beyond the town of Albert. The novelist,
Wilfrid Ewart, recalled "the gathering dusk of leafy lanes and
the twilight of the rolling plains . . . the brilliant weather of the
August days . . . the long, solitary rides, the cool, quiet dusks . . .
the mellow beauty of the harvest times . . . (170)"

*The Somme
nightmare*

Frederic Manning, then a private, remembered marching
back to action: "They sang louder, seeing only the white road

77

before them, and the vague shadows of the trees on either side. At last the singing died away; there was nothing but the tramping of myriad feet; or they would halt for ten minutes, and the darkness along the roadside became alive with fireflies from the glow of cigarettes through a low mist (171)."

Men returned to what Edmund Blunden called "the most terrifying devastated area perhaps yet seen on our planet . . . gunnery had extinguished every sign of life, every step to the horizon and left a specimen of a world without God (172)." Lord Moran, then an army doctor, described the country beyond Delville Wood towards Guillemont. "There was no life, animal or vegetable in the utter desolation of that bleak, charred plain with its black gibbets that were once woods (173)."

For the returning soldiers, it was back to the lottery of death in action. The dead were everywhere. "Other things were left behind," wrote Wyn Griffith, "part of the purchase of this downland, grim disfigured corpses rotting in the sun, so horrible in their discolour that it called for an act of faith to believe that these were once men, young men, sent to their degradation by their fellow men (174)."

There were more attacks on High Wood, Guillemont, Ginchy, recalled by the stunned survivors like terrible dreams. As Frederic Manning described: "The air was ripped by screaming shells, hissing like tons of molten metal plunged suddenly into water . . . and then a face, suddenly an inconceivably distorted face, which raved and sobbed at him as he fell with it into a shell hole . . .

"He closed his eyes and had a vision of men advancing under a rain of shells. They had seemed so toy-like, so trivial and ineffective when opposed to that overwhelming wrath, and yet they moved forward mechanically as though they were hypnotized (175)."

Churchill's memorandum

On both sides, dissatisfaction was growing with the now costly stalemate. In August, Winston Churchill penned a memorandum which attacked the conduct of the Somme offensive – "viewing with the utmost pain, the terrible and disproportionate slaughter of our troops." He shrewdly condemned the conduct of the Battle. "We have not conquered in

Opposite The German fort at Moquet Farm near Pozières – before and after bombardment during August, 1916

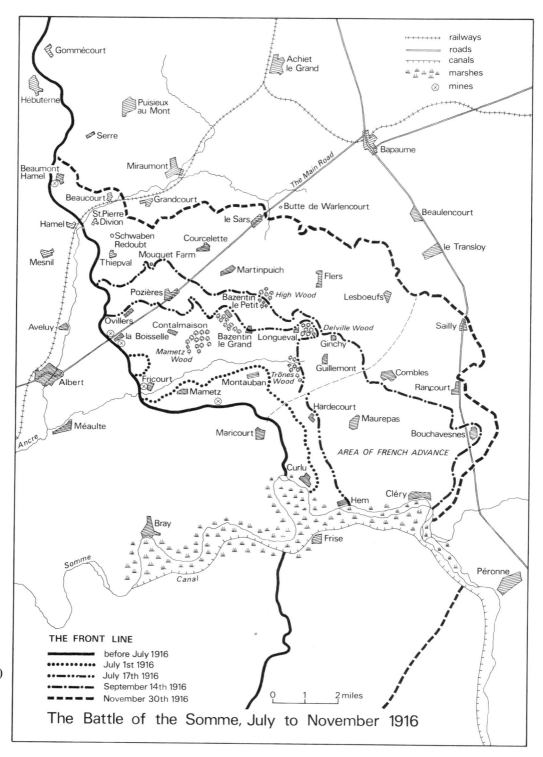

railways
roads
canals
marshes
⊗ mines

Gommécourt

Achiet
le Grand

Hébuterne

Puisieux
au Mont

Serre

Bapaume

Miraumont

Beaumont
Hamel

The Main Road

Beaucourt

Grandcourt

Beaulencourt

Butte de Warlencourt

Hamel

St.Pierre
Divion

le Sars

le Transloy

Schwaben
Redoubt

Courcelette

Mesnil

Thiepval

Mouquet Farm

Martinpuich

Flers

Pozières

Bazentin
le Petit

High Wood

Lesboeufs

Aveluy

Ovillers

Contalmaison

la Boisselle

Bazentin
le Grand

Longueval

Delville Wood

Ginchy

Sailly

Mametz
Wood

Albert

Fricourt

Montauban

Trônes
Wood

Guillemont

Combles

Mametz

Rancourt

Méaulte

Hardecourt

Maurepas

Ancre

Maricourt

Bouchavesnes

AREA OF FRENCH ADVANCE

Curlu

Hem

Cléry

Bray

Frise

Somme

Péronne

Canal

THE FRONT LINE

before July 1916
•••••••• July 1st 1916
—•—•— July 17th 1916
—••—••— September 14th 1916
— — — November 30th 1916

0   1   2 miles

The Battle of the Somme, July to November 1916

80

a month's fighting as much ground as we were expected to gain in the first two hours. We have not advanced two miles in the direct line at any point . . . Unless a gap of at least 20 miles can be opened, no large force can be put through . . . Nor are we making for any point of strategic or political consequence . . . what are Peronne and Bapaume, even if we are likely to take them? The open country towards which we are struggling by inches is capable of entrenched defence at every step and is utterly devoid of military significance. There is no question of breaking the line, of 'letting loose the cavalry' in the open country behind or of inducing a general withdrawal of the German armies in the West . . . In personnel," he concluded, "the results of the operation have been disastrous; in terrain they have been absolutely barren (176)."

General Robertson, Chief of the Imperial General Staff, wrote to Haig from London, "the powers-that-be are beginning to get a little uneasy . . . The casualties are mounting up and they are wondering whether we are likely to get a proper return for them (177)." Haig wrote back, justifying his results: "Pressure on Verdun relieved . . . proof given to the world that the Allies are capable of making and maintaining a vigorous offensive and of driving the enemy's best troops from the strongest positions . . . we have inflicted very heavy losses on the enemy." He concluded that "the maintenance of a steady offensive pressure will result in his [the German's] complete overthrow." But he admitted that "it would not be justifiable to calculate on the enemy's being completely broken without another campaign next year (178)." Angry at the "cabal of sacked generals" in London, he began planning a third major Somme offensive. He also relieved his feelings by blaming junior officers for "want of thorough preparations" in planning attacks during August. *Haig's defence*

For the Germans, too, the Somme had become "that terrible conflict," "this cancer in the West." At the end of August, the Kaiser replaced Falkenhayn with Field-Marshal von Hindenberg. General Ludendorff became his deputy. The failure of Falkenhayn's Verdun offensive contrasted unfavourably with Hindenberg's successes on the Eastern Front. In early September, the two "new brooms" travelled to Cambrai to consider *New German leaders*

A soldier surveys German corpses in a machine gun post destroyed by
British shell fire

the Western Front. "The loss of ground up to date appeared to
me of little importance in itself," wrote Ludendorff. "We could
stand that, but the question how this and the progressive falling
off of our fighting power of which it was symptomatic was to be
prevented, was of immense importance . . . My mental picture
of the fighting at Verdun and on the Somme had to be painted
a shade darker in view of what I had just heard (179)."

The Germans on the Somme were promised more guns,
ammunition and aircraft for what Hindenberg called "The
Battle of Material." The deep dugouts – death traps now – were
to be given up; a new flexible defence system based on "pillbox"
forts was to be developed. A new, very strong defence line, the
Siegfried Stellung or Hindenberg Line, was begun some miles to

the rear of the Somme front. Hindenberg declared: "The plan of the Entente [Britain and France] to overwhelm us once and for all in the autumn of 1916 . . . was foiled for the time being (180)."

In Britain, during August, the public were able to see the official film, "The Battle of the Somme." It caused a sensation and marked a new stage in the presentation of war to the home front, as the photographs of the Crimea or the American Civil War had done in the previous century. The film showed the preparations for battle, men waiting to attack, troops leaping over the parapet, prisoners and wounded coming in. King George V commented, "The public should see these pictures." The public went in thousands. *The Somme film*

In London, the critic of *The Nation,* noted the significance of the new vision of war. "The Cinema . . . shows for the first time scenes which have actually happened during a war from one moment to the next . . . There is the thing itself; this is what men really did . . . that was the look on their faces as they went to death; there is the cigarette still smoking. What would we not give for a glimpse of the thin line springing to advance when Wellington waved his hat at Waterloo? Perhaps a time may come when this finest of cinemas may be brought out from the British Museum on special days as a historic curiosity (181)."

There was equal interest in the provinces. A review in a Cambridge local paper praised the film, with warm words for the pianist who provided the background music. "Stirring war songs are played as the troops sway past on their march into battle and, a moment later, as the dead heroes are seen lying in the field, 'The Flowers of the Forest' is most feelingly rendered . . . One comes from 'The Battle of the Somme' . . . conscious of coming victory; calm in the sure knowledge that the German eagle has matched its strength with the British lion and failed (182)."

The age of the artist illustrator and his romantic pictures of war was over. The grainy, jerky sequences of the Somme film showed "what kind of a bestial horror the war has become."

A British Mark I tank waiting to attack Gueudecourt. Note the British
soldiers' interest in the new weapon, the "dazzle" camouflage and the
cavalry in the background

7 The First Tanks: "The Devil is Coming"

IN EARLY SEPTEMBER, the capture of the village ruins of Guillemont and Ginchy on the right flank, allowed Haig to consider a new general advance. This time he would use a new weapon – the tank.

The need for such a "landship" or "land iron-clad" had been pondered since the beginning of the century. A Boer War (1899–1902) correspondent noted, "The quick firing rifle has changed the face of war. The great question is to provide cover for troops in action (183)." H. G. Wells wrote an influential story, "The Land Ironclads," describing a huge, crawling machine that was "something between a big block house and a giant's dish-cover." *The tank*

The trench stalemate led to renewed interest in the idea of "artificial cover." Winston Churchill, First Sea Lord, was always keen on new ideas. He set up a "Landships Committee" at the Admiralty in 1915. Churchill wrote to Prime Minister Asquith about the idea. "Forty or fifty of these machines prepared secretly . . . could advance into the enemy trenches, smashing away all obstructions and sweeping the trenches with their machine-gun fire . . . They would then make so many *'points d'appui'* [rallying points] for the British supporting infantry to rush forward and rally on them (184)."

At the same time, a Lt. Col. Swinton wrote to the War Office advocating "petrol driven tractors on the caterpillar principle . . . armoured with hardened steel plates . . . and armed with – say – two maxims and a maxim two pounder gun" to break the trench lines (185).

85

By June, 1915, a Joint Services Committee had prepared an actual specification. In January, 1916, the first machine, nicknamed "Mother," was crossing nine-foot trenches in tests. Despite the doubts of Kitchener, who commented, "a pretty mechanical toy," 100 machines were ordered. The secrecy surrounding the project called for a disguise name. Among those proposed – "container," "cistern," "water carrier" – "tank" seemed the best.

Churchill, by then an officer in France, sent a paper to Headquarters, describing "the caterpillars" and their potential. Haig was curious. "Is anything known about the caterpillars referred to?" he wrote to London. His haste to have the machines ready for his planned offensive on the Somme worried the tank pioneers. Swinton warned: "Since the chance of success of any attack by tanks lies almost entirely in its novelty . . . these machines *should not be used in driblets* . . . [we must wait] until the whole are ready to be launched together with the infantry assault in one great combined operation (186)."

The tanks come to France

However, plans went ahead to rush the machines into action. Tank crews began training on Thetford Heath in Norfolk. Eight men were crammed into the unlit, box-like interior, stifled with fumes from exhaust and from the guns, and deafened by the engine roar. The tanks, labelled in Russian "to Petrograd with care," were shipped to France in September, 1916. With their strange, dazzle-paint camouflage, they were a sensation to the troops. The ill-trained crews were soon exhausted by demonstrations, as were the untried machines. After breakdown, only 32 tanks could actually go into battle on 15th September, and only 18 of these were really useful in action.

The battle plan

The battle plan was the same as 1st July on a smaller scale. If a gap was broken between "The Road" and Morval village, five divisions of cavalry would ride through into open country. Lloyd George, who visited the Front at this time, was sceptical of this plan. "When I ventured to express to Generals Joffre and Haig my doubts as to whether cavalry could ever operate successfully on a front bristling for miles behind the enemy line with barbed wire and machine-guns, both generals fell ecstatically on me . . . The conversation gave me an idea of the exaltation

Opposite Stretcher bearers silhouetted against the sunset bring in the dead and wounded from the Somme battlefield

produced in brave men by battle. They were quite incapable of looking beyond and around or even through the struggle just in front of them . . . (187)"

Last thoughts

As the three-day preliminary bombardment roared from "Happy Valley," doomed soldiers, like Captain T. M. Kettle, wrote last letters home. "I am calm and happy but desperately anxious to live . . . the big guns are coughing and smacking their shells, which sound for all the world like overhead express trains . . . Somewhere the Choosers of the Slain are touching as in our Norse story they used to touch with invisible wands those who are to die . . . (188)"

German shock

The tanks were used singly to assist in capturing strongpoints. Advancing with the infantry at 6.20 on the morning of 15th September, they gave the Germans a fearsome surprise. A German journalist described how they saw "mysterious monsters . . . crawling towards them over the craters . . . The monsters approached slowly, hobbling, rolling and rocking but they approached. Nothing impeded them: a supernatural force seemed to impel them on. Someone in the trenches said, 'The Devil is coming,' and the word was passed along the line like wild fire (189)."

Inside the tanks

To the men inside, it was hot and claustrophobic. One reported: "Hun bullets are rebounding from our tough sides like

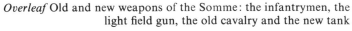

Overleaf Old and new weapons of the Somme: the infantrymen, the light field gun, the old cavalry and the new tank

87

hail from a glass roof. We just crawl over the embankment, guns and all . . . Two or three Huns are brave enough to creep on the back of the tank from behind. We open a small trapdoor and shoot them with a revolver . . . A large lyddite bomb bursts against the armoured jacket of my gun. The flare comes in through the porthole, blinding me for a minute or two, while splinters strike my face (190)."

On the left, the Canadians seized Courcellette; Scottish troops were successful at Martinpuich, and High Wood was finally captured. The tanks had their greatest success at Flers, where one tank drove up the main street, to the surprise of its German defenders. The village surrendered and a British pilot signalled back a confusing message: "A tank is walking up the High Street of Flers with the British Army cheering behind (191)." The crest of the ridge had been won. The gap, it seemed, had opened. *Tank success*

But the attack on the right was unsuccessful. By afternoon, the breach was again sealed. Dusk fell on a battlefield novel in appearance only because of the hulks of abandoned tanks that littered it. Haig had been impressed by the machines: "Wherever the tanks advanced we took our objectives." Orders for a thousand tanks were placed. The tank pioneers were depressed. "This priceless conception," wrote Churchill, "was revealed to the Germans for the mere petty purpose of taking a few ruined villages (192)."

On 25th September, the advance continued: Morval and Lesboeufs were captured, Gueudecourt and Combles abandoned by the Germans. On the 26th, Thiepval itself fell at last. Adrian Stephen watched from across the valley. "Then with a plunge the first wave [of troops] . . . vanished amidst the ruined houses . . . More brown figures streamed across the open. A black dog ran out of a dugout to meet them; a man stooped and fondled it. When they draw near to the line of chalk heaps, I saw black masses emerge . . . Prisoners were giving themselves up without a fight . . . Thiepval was now a closed book (193)." *Capture of Thiepval*

Captured letters reveal the sufferings of German soldiers during these months of battle. "Hans is dead. Fritz is dead. Wilhelm is dead. There are many dead . . . this is almost un-

Opposite Support troops leave their trench to follow the first waves in their successful attack on Morval, 25th September, 1916

endurable (194)."

Failure

Nonetheless, a last German line still stretched intact before the Allies. A British officer, soon to die, wrote of the Battle at this point, "One can compare . . . our whole offensive to a little boy who sets out to climb a big tree. On failing to reach the first bough, he takes out a pocketknife and proceeds to cut it down. That is what we are doing. On the 26th, the tree, after three months of cutting, was showing a little weakness through loss of sap (195)."

*The suffering
of the Somme*

A drowsy mood fell over the battlefield; the Battle was really over. The writer A. D. Gristwood described a captured German trench. "Sometimes the Germans had buried their dead in the floor of the trench, where, baking in the sun, the earth had cracked into starshaped fissures. A foot treading unwarily here sank suddenly downwards, disturbing hundreds of white and wriggling maggots. In one place, a hand with blue and swollen fingers projected helplessly from the ground. 'O death, where is thy sting? O Grave, where is thy victory?' (196)"

A single corpse was a symbol of the agony of the Battle. "Close to the trench, a man . . . stood nearly upright, buried to the waist, his arms fast bound to his sides, his glassy eyes wide open to the sky, his face stained a livid yellow from the fumes of an explosion. Who he was nobody knew . . . he stood, glaring upwards as though mutely appealing from Earth to Heaven (197)."

*Press
comment on
tanks*

The Press in Britain celebrated the September victories. The tank caused particular interest. It was described as "land dreadnought," "half battleship, half caterpillar," "touring fort," "flat footed monster" or "giant, polychromatic toad" – even as "a jabberwock with eyes of flame." As no photographs were published until December, newspaper artists had to guess what the tank looked like. The favourite tone in Press reports was comedy. In Philip Gibbs's report, a "cockney soldier" described the tanks. "They broke down trees as if they were matchsticks, and went over barricades like elephants. The Boche [Germans] were thoroughly scared. They came running out of shell holes and trenches shouting like mad things. Some of them attacked the tanks and tried to bomb them but it wasn't a bit of good.

O Crikey! It was a rare treat to see! The biggest joke that ever was! (198)"

These reports coincided with the R.F.C.'s spectacular victories against the Zeppelin over London. The defending aeroplanes, now equipped with incendiary bullets, scored the first success on 2nd September. A Shutte-Lanz airship was shot down in blazing ruin by Second-Lieutenant Leefe Robinson, who won the Victoria Cross. On the 23rd another Zeppelin, one of a large bombing force, was destroyed by a Lieutenant Sowrey. He later recalled, "The airship was well lighted by searchlights . . . I could distinctly see the propellers revolving, and the airship was manoeuvring to avoid the searchlight beams. I fired at it . . . [and] caused the envelope to catch fire in several places . . . I

R.F.C. victories

An artist's fantastic idea of the tanks. No photograph of them was published until December, 1916, so speculative illustration ran riot

watched the burning airship strike the ground and then proceeded to fire my flares (199)."

To Londoners, the tremendous spectacle in the sky was a focus for their revenge against the raiders. Michael Macdonagh saw the burning Zeppelin. "My attention was attracted by frenzied cries of 'Oh, she's hit' . . . I saw high in the sky . . . a ruddy glow which rapidly spread into the outline of a blazing airship . . . The Zeppelin drifted perpendicularly in the darkened sky, a gigantic pyramid of flames, red and orange, like a ruined star falling slowly to earth. Its glare lit up the streets and gave a ruddy tint even to the waters of the Thames . . . when at last the doomed airship vanished from sight, there arose a shout, the like of which I have never heard in London before – a hoarse shout of mingled execration, triumph and joy, a swelling shout that appeared to be rising from all parts of the metropolis . . . It was London's '*Te Deum*' for another crowning deliverance (200)."

The wreck, which fell in Essex, became a magnet for fascinated crowds. Macdonagh joined them. "In the distance I could see the huge aluminium framework of the wrecked airship gleaming brightly in the sunshine . . . It is like the skeleton of a monstrous prehistoric reptile, the aluminium girders, corroded by fire, suggesting the bleached bones (201)."

Other Zeppelins were shot down in October and November. The celebrations were premature, as the Germans now began bombing with the less vulnerable aeroplane. The victory over the Zeppelins, like the autumn "victories" on the Somme, marked only the end of the beginning, not the beginning of the end.

8 "The Land of Despair": The End of the Battle

IN OCTOBER, Haig continued to attack the last German defences in front of the town of Bapaume. Having struggled to the top of the ridge, his men now struggled down the other side, lengthening their communications over the shattered field. They were to spend the winter in flooded trenches. The fine weather broke on 2nd October, turning the field into a sea of mud. The Official History commented, "Conditions on and behind the battlefront were so bad as to make mere existence a severe trial of body and spirit."

The Somme mud, clinging to the men's feet in huge balls, now seemed the greatest enemy. "It was like walking in caramel," wrote an officer, Sidney Rogerson. "Distances were measured not in yards, but in mud (202)."

The autumn landscape was desolate, "drab and formless as one imagines Earth must have been before the appearance of life." Max Plowman, a junior officer who later became a writer, recalled the dreary scene. "There appear, in countless succession . . . shell holes filled with water. The sense of desolation these innumerable, silent, circular pools produce is horrible. So vividly do they remind me of a certain illustration by Doré to Dante's 'Inferno' that I begin to wonder whether I have not stepped out of life and entered one of the circles of the damned; and as I look upon these evil pools I half expect to see a head appearing from each one (203)." *Desolate landscapes*

Conditions in the front line were scarcely tolerable. "Who ever it is we are relieving, they are gone already," went on Plowman. "The trench is empty. In the watery moonlight, it

95

appears a very ghostly place. Corpses lie along the parados, rotting in the wet: every now and then a booted foot appears jutting over the trench. The mud makes it all but impassable (204)." Even a stolid regular officer, like Graham Greenwell, protested, "This is a disgusting hole: if only the people at home could imagine a tenth of the vileness of this part of the world that figures so gloriously in all our cold official communiqués . . . We have been here for thirty-six hours now, living like dogs or rats . . . We think mud, dream mud and eat mud (205)."

The Butte of Warlencourt   Any gains the soldiers made were really meaningless. One landmark in the area was an ancient burial mound, the Butte of Warlencourt. The men were unable to capture it until November. "The Butte [mound] seemed to tower over you and threaten you with its hidden machine gun posts," wrote Charles Carrington. It was "a monstrosity," "lifting its pale back in the murk, an awful monster prone in solitude (206)." The Butte and Le Sars village were tide marks of the British advance towards Bapaume.

For tired, wet soldiers even the march out of the line was an agony. One soldier reported: "On either side of the track, exhausted men of the incoming division were lying slowly

German cavalrymen wait to go up the line during the German retreat on the Somme

drowning in the mud. What could you do except give them the contents of your flask? (207)"

Left of the field beyond the village of Thiepval was the ridge overlooking the River Ancre. The troops had to capture Thiepval before carrying out a planned final strike at Beaumont-Hamel. Edmund Blunden caught the atmosphere of this sector. "It was now approaching the beginning of November and the days were melancholy and the colour of clay. We took over that death-trap known as the Schwaben Redoubt . . . Crossing the Ancre again . . . one immediately entered the land of despair . . . the shell holes were mostly small lakes of what was no doubt merely rusty water, but had a red and foul resemblance to blood. Paths glistened weakly from tenable point to point. Of the dead, one was conspicuous. He was a Scottish soldier, and was kneeling, facing east, so that one could scarcely credit death to him . . . Death could not kneel so, I thought, but approaching it I ascertained with a sudden shrivelling of spirit that Death could and did (208)." *Horrors of Thiepval*

When at last this ridge was taken, the attack on the Ancre Valley could begin. The Germans, assuming that the Battle was over, were taken by surprise. On 13th November, in a heavy fog, the attack began. A two-pronged infantry movement was launched on Beaumont-Hamel and the tunnelled ruins of St. Pierre Divion over the river. After five days, both villages were captured. Only the "sinister ruins" of Serre remained impregnable. The German General Ludendorff described this last advance as "a particularly heavy blow." *Last Somme attacks*

On 18th November, the last attacks beyond Beaucourt took place in the winter's first snow storms. The Official History recorded the close of the Battle. "The infantry, dark figures only visible for a short distance against the white ground, groped their way forward as best they could through half frozen mud that was soon to dissolve into chalky slime. Little wonder that direction was often lost and with it the precious barrage, while the objectives, mantled in snow, were hard indeed to identify (209)."

Perhaps the most significant event of the last month of the Battle was when an obscure German soldier was wounded in

D

The desolation at the end of the Battle: a tank stranded in the mud at Thiepval, November, 1916

the leg near Bapaume. Had the shell killed him, history would have been changed. The German recalled: "For us the impression created was that of a veritable inferno, rather than war. Through weeks of incessant artillery bombardment we stood firm, at times ceding a little ground but then taking it back again . . . On 7th October, 1916, I was wounded but had the luck of being able to get back to our lines . . . (210)" This man was Adolf Hitler, who was to invalidate single-handed the result of the entire war.

End of the Battle   The Battle, that Asquith called "the long and sombre procession of cruelty and suffering," came to an end. The journalist, H. M. Tomlinson, recorded a last image of its suffering. "A boy's alabaster face . . . hung backwards out of a heap of trash, what was left of his fair hair washed flat by rain, his eyes open to the indifferent sky, and his mouth gaping in astonishment and pain that belonged to the past (211)."

Protest: war poets   As the Battle ended, the voice of protest began to be heard. A minority of soldiers expressed their horror at "the unspeakable

Opposite The last victories: a muddy success near Serre in November, 1916

agonies of the Somme.'' A New Army sergeant, Leslie Coulson, killed in October, recorded his anguish in his last poem (212).

Who made the Law that men should die in meadows?
Who spake the word that blood should splash in lanes?
Who gave it forth that gardens should be boneyards?
Who spread the hills with flesh, and blood and brains?
                    Who made the law?
. . . But who made the law? The trees shall whisper to him:
"See, see the blood – the splashes on our bark!"
Walking the meadows, he shall hear bones crackle
And fleshless mouths shall gibber in silent lanes at dark.
                    Who made the law?

The fighting at Mametz Wood caused a grim outburst from the poet Robert Graves (213).

Today I found in Mametz Wood
A certain cure for lust of blood:

Where propped against a shattered trunk,
In a great mess of things unclean,
Sat a dead Boche; he scowled and stunk,
With clothes and face a sodden green,
Big-bellied, spectacled, crop-haired,
Dribbling black blood from nose and beard.

The same fighting also brought a haunting sketch from Siegfried Sassoon, about the last ravings of a wounded soldier (214).

The ward grew dark; but he was still complaining
And calling out for "Dickie! Curse the Wood!
It's time to go. O Christ, and what's the good?
We'll never take it, and it's always raining!"
I wondered where he'd been; then heard him shout,
"They snipe like hell! O Dickie, don't go out . . ."
I fell asleep . . . next morning he was dead . . .

"All the horror of the Somme attacks was in that raving; all the darkness and the dreadful daylight, . . . " commented Sassoon (215).

Bertrand Russell, the philosopher, set out his anti-war opinions in his essays, *Justice in War Time*. "The real motive which prolongs the war is pride. Is there no statesman who can think in terms of Europe, not only of separate nations? Is our civilization a thing of no account to all our rulers? . . . I hope that somewhere among the men who hold power in Europe there is at least one who will remember . . . that we are the guardians not only of the nation, but of that common heritage of thought and art and a humane way of life into which we were born, but which our children may find wasted by our blind violence and hate (216)." Russell's support of conscientious objectors led to his prosecution under D.O.R.A. *Bertrand Russell*

The voice of protest also had an eloquent outlet in *The Nation*, a weekly periodical edited by H. W. Massingham. One of his editorials discussed the effect of violence on society: "Force has taken a new place in our lives and transformed our outlook in subtle and manifold ways that defy analysis. The return to the civilian mind, to persuasion, to government by frank and tolerant opinion will nowhere be easy (217)." *The Nation*

In an article called "Pale for Weariness," Massingham described the effect of war on Europe at the end of 1916. "Europe is tired out . . . not only is the best blood of Europe being spilled without ceasing in the trenches but the vitality of the remaining millions is being immeasurably drained by the constant demand for guns, for shells, and for supplies . . . Millions are being racked by anxiety as to a loved one's fate . . . The Europe of the Great Peace will be a sickly and enfeebled continent: the flower of its youth will have withered where it grew, and the spring

101

will have vanished from its year. Pale from the loss of blood will our new world be; pale also for weariness (218)."

Lastly there was pressure for a negotiated peace from within the Government itself. In November, 1916, a Memorandum was circulated within the Cabinet by Lord Lansdowne, Minister without Portfolio. He foresaw social and economic disaster if the war continued. "What does prolongation of the war mean? Our own casualties already amount to over 1,100,000. We have had 15,000 officers killed . . . We are slowly but surely killing off the best of the male population of these islands . . . The financial burden which we have already accumulated is almost incalculable. We are adding to it at the rate of £5,000,000 a day. Generations will have to come and go before the country recovers from the loss . . . Can we afford to go on paying the same price for the same sort of gain? (219)"

Such protests received little sympathy in 1916. As the sufferings of war increased, attitudes hardened. Sylvia Pankhurst described how pacifist meetings were broken up. "Poorly clad women with pinched, white faces and backs bent by excessive toil, their eyes flashing and fists clenched, rushed out from their hovels screaming, 'No peace without victory! We want peace on *our* terms!' . . . Saddest of all were the degraded, the starved and shabby, who rushed intoxicated from the public houses . . . demanding that the entire German population should be 'wiped out!' Sometimes they would attempt a tipsy war dance in the midst of our crowd . . . (220)."

The conscientious objectors bore the brunt of public hostility. They were tongue lashed by the chairmen of Tribunals. "A man who would not help defend his own country and womankind is a coward and a cad. You are nothing but a shivering mass of unwholesome fat." Lloyd George led the campaign against them with the chill promise, "I shall consider the best means of making the lot of that class a hard one."

The minority of "absolutist" objectors, who refused any war service, were sometimes subjected to considerable brutality. Some were even shipped to France, where refusal to obey orders meant the death penalty. The scandal about these men caused the *Daily News* to ask, "Where are we drifting?"

9 The Results of the Battle

NO ONE KNOWS exactly how many men became casualties on the Somme. The official figures set the British Empire total at 419,654; the French at 204,253. The German figures, based on lost records, total some 500,000. Over a million men from the three armies involved were killed, wounded or captured on the Somme. In return a small slice of France, twenty-five miles long and seven miles deep at most, had changed hands.

Somme casualties

This vast human catastrophe shook national leaders in all three countries: Falkenhayn had gone in Germany; Joffre lost his command in France; Asquith, the British Prime Minister, broken by the death of his son in the Battle, was replaced by Lloyd George. Haig survived to plan the costly, ineffective battles of 1917.

Propagandists became busy exalting the "Sacrifice" of the Somme. John Buchan, whose book on the Battle was intended for the American market, wrote, "The young men who died almost before they had looked on the world, the makers and doers who left their tasks unfinished were greater in their deaths than in their lives . . . Their memory will abide so long as men are found to set honour before ease, and a nation lives not for its ledgers alone but for some purpose of virtue (221)."

The "Sacrifice"

Horatio Bottomley, editor of *John Bull*, took this idea further. "They who have fallen in battle fighting consciously for the Right are now with the immortals – though their sins were as scarlet, their souls are as white as snow . . . (222)"

The versifier, John Oxenham, whose "helpful verse for these dark days of war" brought him considerable profit, provided

Overleaf A dead German found at Beaumont-Hamel, November, 1916

"comfort" for the bereaved (223).

> *Unnamed at times, at times unknown,*
> *Our graves lie thick beyond the seas;*
> *Unnamed but not of Him unknown:*
> *He knows! He sees!*
>
> *. . . The world was sinking in a slough*
> *Of sloth, and ease, and selfish greed;*
> *God surely sent this scourge to mould*
> *A nobler creed . . .*

Winston Churchill's epitaph

Winston Churchill wrote the best-balanced epitaph for the British dead of the Somme, especially those from Kitchener's New Armies: "The finest we have ever marshalled, improvised at the sound of the cannonade, every man a volunteer, inspired not only by love of country but by a widespread conviction that human freedom was challenged by military and Imperial tyranny, they grudged no sacrifice, however unfruitful, and shrank from no ordeal however destructive. Struggling forward through the mire and filth of the trenches, across the corpse-strewn crater-fields, amid the flaring, crashing, blasting barrages and murderous machine-gun fire . . . they seized the most formidable soldiery of Europe by the throat, slew them and hurled them unceasingly backward . . . The battlefields of the Somme were the graveyards of Kitchener's Army. The flower of that generous manhood . . . which came at the call of Britain . . . was shorn away for ever in 1916 (224)."

Haig's claims

Haig liked to claim the Somme as a victory. In his despatch of 23rd December, 1916, he disregarded his original breakthrough plan and claimed that he had wanted a battle of attrition. His aims had been, he said, to relieve pressure on Verdun, to wear down the strength of the German armies and to help Britain's Allies by engaging German troops. "Anyone of these three results is in itself sufficient to justify the Somme Battle. The attainment of all of them affords ample compensation for the splendid efforts of our troops and for the sacrifices made by ourselves and our Allies. They have brought us a long step forward towards the final victory of the Allied cause (225)." Haig's denial of his breakthrough plan was described by Liddell-Hart as "one of the most elaborate perversions of historical truth that has come to light (226)."

It was true that the German General Ludendorff confessed *A draw* that his "army had been fought to a standstill and was utterly worn out" by the end of the Battle. He had advised: "We must spare the troops a second Somme Battle (227)." But the Germans had held the formidable Franco-British thrust, and the attackers were exhausted by November. Perhaps the Somme is best seen as a draw between evenly matched opponents. Robert Graves had seen in Mametz Wood a vivid symbol of this: there were "two unforgettable corpses: a man of the South Wales Borderers and one of the Lehr Regiment had succeeded in bayoneting each other simultaneously (228)."

The Somme was historically important because it marked the first large-scale British commitment to a European land war for a century. Half a million British soldiers were casualties on the Western Front up to 30th June, 1916; over two million afterwards. Seventy three percent of the huge cost of the war for Britain (£8,742,000,000) was incurred after 1st July, 1916.

The Battle also saw the beginning of new methods of warfare. *A turning* The bayonet charge and the glamorous cavalry were remnants *point* of nineteenth century war; the machine gun, the artillery, the tank and the aeroplane were portents of the new age. "From then onwards," wrote the poet, David Jones, of 1916, "things hardened into a more relentless, mechanical affair, took on a more sinister aspect . . . (229)"

Faith in authority, belief in God were severely shaken by the horrors of the 1914–18 battles. Twentieth century cynicism and desolation of spirit were born among the shell holes and shattered skeleton trees of fields like the Somme.

The high hopes and crushing sorrows of the summer and autumn of 1916 make the Battle live on in popular memory. In contrast, the sweeping Allied victories of 1918 over the same ground are half-forgotten, although Haig then reconquered the entire Somme battlefield in one weekend. *The Times* then commented, "These are great days . . . when one remembers what the names of Thiepval and Fricourt and Mametz and Contalmaison meant in the old days of 1916 . . . it is difficult to realize that we have again swept over all that ground between Friday

night and Sunday morning (230)."

After the fighting was over in 1916, winter descended on the desolate Battle area. Survivors, like Henry Williamson, could explore the desolation and remember the summer. "A brass buckle; a fragment of leather; skull with curls matted upon it; puttee coiled about leg-bone; broken helmet from which sandbag covering had fretted away, leaving only the faded paint of divisional colours – everywhere the dead had merged with the ground. Where was Rose Avenue? He was lost, helplessly in chalky waste. Ovillers was a disturbed whiteness, a frozen sea with thin, black masts . . . the summer print of faces and places faded in the cold ruin of winter . . . Thousands upon thousands of helmets lay among the grass bents and thistle stalks. Anguish rose in him: wherever he looked, to whatever horizon . . . the grey wilderness extended in an arc of skyline fretted by stumps of trees . . . (231)" *Winter, 1916–17*

Later, during a notoriously cold winter, snow covered the wasteland. Wilfred Owen, the war poet, came to the trenches for the first time on the downs near Beaumont-Hamel. He wrote, "We were marooned on a frozen desert. There is not a sign of life on the horizon, and a thousand signs of death. Not a blade of grass, not an insect; once or twice a day, the shadow of a big hawk, scenting carrion (232)."

In February, 1917, the Germans withdrew to their new defence system, the Hindenberg Line. They gave up nearly 1,000 square miles of French territory, which they left systematically devastated. The German commanders thus shortened their trench line by 32 miles. To the British, this seemed further proof of a Somme victory. "It caused a great falling back of the enemy armies," wrote John Masefield. "It first gave the enemy the knowledge that he was beaten (233)." *The Hindenberg Line*

Masefield toured the Somme battlefields in early 1917 to collect material for his book, *The Old Front Line*. Near the Schwaben Redoubt at Thiepval he observed, "The ground is littered with relics of our charges; mouldy packs, old shattered scabbards, rifles, bayonets, helmets, curled, torn, rolled and scarred, clips of cartridges and very many graves. Many . . . are marked with strips of wood from packing cases, with pencilled *The Old Front Line*

109

Opposite "To Your Health, Civilization" by the cartoonist Louis Raemaekers. Death drinks a toast in blood after reaping a huge harvest in the war during 1916

inscriptions, 'An Unknown British hero' . . . 'a dead Fritz.' That gentle slope to the Schwaben is covered with such things (234)."

Near Hamel he saw more British dead. "There are many English graves (marked then, hurriedly, by the man's rifle thrust into the ground) in that piece of line. On a windy day, these rifles shook in the wind as the bayonets beat to the blast. The field testaments of both men lay open beside them in the mud . . . [one of them] was open at the eighty-ninth Psalm and the only legible words were 'Thou hast broken down all his hedges; Thou hast brought his strongholds to ruin' (235)."

William Orpen

In summer, 1917, William Orpen, one of the Official War artists, came to paint the old, devastated area. "Never shall I forget my first sight of the Somme in summertime . . . No words could express the beauty of it. The dreary, dismal mud was baked white and pure – dazzling white. White daisies, red poppies and a blue flower, great masses of them, stretched for miles and miles. The sky a pure, dark blue, and the whole air . . . thick with white butterflies; your clothes were covered with butterflies. It was an enchanted land: but in place of fairies, there were thousands of little white crosses marked 'Unknown British soldier' . . . blue dragonflies darted about; high up the larks sang; higher still the aeroplanes droned. Everything shimmered in the heat . . . (236)"

1918 battles

However, the following spring was to see the Germans again crossing this wasteland after the breakthrough of their March offensives. The Golden Virgin of Albert at last fell from its spire; the town itself was captured. Again the Allies pressed the Germans back, and another mass of white crosses sprang up on the Somme battlefield before peace finally came in 1918.

The Somme memorials

In the 1920s life returned to the district. The British dead were gathered into fifty cemeteries; the Germans were grudgingly allowed one, at Fricourt. The ugly monuments were proudly set up, including the sinister arch at Thiepval where the names of 73,412 men who *disappeared* on the Somme are recorded. Thoughtful visitors and old soldiers made the pilgrimage to Picardy.

The American novelist, F. Scott Fitzgerald, described a visit to the trenches at Beaumont-Hamel, preserved as a memorial.

In his *Tender is the Night* he gave a final comment on the waste and futility of the Battle of the Somme, and the war itself.

"Dick turned the corner of the traverse and continued along the trench, walking on the duckboard . . . Then he got up on the step and peered over the parapet. In front of him, beneath a dingy sky, was Beaumont-Hamel; to his left, the tragic hill of Thiepval . . .

"'This land here cost twenty lives a foot that summer," he said to Rosemary . . . 'See that little stream? We could walk to it in two minutes. It took the British a month to walk to it, a whole Empire walking very slowly, dying in front and pushing forward behind. And another Empire walking very slowly backward a few inches a day, leaving the dead like a million bloody rugs. . .' (237)"

Epilogue: The Lost Generation

THE PHRASE, "The Lost Generation," used in the 1920s to describe the war dead, was based on statistical fact. Over three-quarters of a million British soldiers died in the war; nearly two million more were seriously wounded. The casualty rate was worst among junior officers: 37,452 died in France and Flanders. These men were the cream of their generation.

Contemporaries were at first pleasantly surprised at the way young men went willingly to die for their country. The *New Statesmen* commented in 1916: "In the present war, men go voluntarily to death in a manner that has amazed all who held that the European races had grown decadent and had lost their courage . . . Obviously thousands of young men are living in the spirit of Achilles. There is nothing in the record of human warfare – no, not the glory of Marathon or Thermopylae – to surpass this epic of courage and self sacrifice that is being written all over the face of Europe today . . . (238)"

Shrewder writers were horrified at the waste of lives. H. W. Massingham wrote in *The Nation*: "In every country it is the officer class . . . that yields the heaviest percentage of killed . . . They are, on the whole, the intellectual elite of the middle class and among the working class the men most worthy of responsibility and command. Some men of known genius and talent are among them, here a Rupert Brooke and a Raymond Asquith, and there a Prof. Kettle and for everyone of these, scores of hundreds of youths whose capacity promised service or fame . . . The loss of talent, knowledge and character must be ever more appalling and for a generation we must expect an appreciable impoverishment of leadership as the weeded ranks come to middle age in the arts, in political and social life and in commerce. For it is, on the whole, the generous, the ardent, the enterprising who fall in the largest numbers, and the cautious, the selfish and the timid who survive. Within a nation, war inverts the natural process of the survival of the fittest (239)."

Gerard Garvin was a young officer killed on the Somme in late July, 1916. His story, reconstructed from his letters, diary and notebooks, expresses the tragedy of "The Lost Generation." He was the only son of J. L. Garvin (1868–1947), the famous editor of *The Observer* from 1908–42. He had revitalized the paper and made it a centre of interest in British political life. By 1914 he was a man of great influence, near the centre of power.

His son, born in 1896, had left Westminster School to go to Oxford. The war had intervened and instead he went to enlist in the South Lancashire Regiment. While he trained and was sent to France (June, 1915), his father wrote and spoke supporting the war and the necessity for a military victory to crush "Prussianism."

By June, 1916, Gerard was on the Staff at his Divisional Headquarters on the Somme. In his daily letters to his father, he recorded his surroundings quite sensitively. "How one loves the lines of trees in the valleys, elm and white poplar, and the windmills . . . I had a jolly walk last night round the village and back through the wood behind the château. The moon was full and bright in the twilight, and the crops yellowing, except for one silver field of oats. A big owl swept over my head, silently with long wings spread out. I could hear the clangour of artillery and see distant flashes occasionally (240)." He collected flowers from a trench top to send to his mother.

When the Somme Battle began, he briefly recorded his impressions in a field notebook.

"Saturday, 24th June. Bombardment begins in the morning. No sound. Flashes and Very lights at night, faint sounds . . .

"30th June . . . Day quiet . . . Fine evening, sunset of flare fading through rose and grey violet to darkness . . . Night dark but clear with bright starlight.

"Saturday, 1st July. 'Z' day. Delicious summer morning.

Thick mist. Shattering bombardment on waking. Can see very little from hill. Hear continuous roar from left . . . News comes along very slowly. Tense expectation . . . (241)"

Following the death in action of a close friend, he was transferred at his own request to the front to share real battle experience. Not seeing the casualties, people at home were impressed by the progress of the Battle. On 17th July, his father wrote to him, "That second offensive of Friday and Saturday was a splendid feat. The whole thing seems to have gone like clockwork . . . When we let fly again, we shall be on the crown of the country between the Ancre and the Somme . . . There will be nothing ahead of us on the Bapaume–Peronne sector quite so formidable . . . (242)"

At the front, things seemed much less confident. The Battle now became attrition fighting. On 21st July, the attack was resumed. At 11.30 p.m., on the night of 23rd July, Gerard Garvin was killed in action near Bazentin-Le-Petit. His orderly was beside him and described his death. "I can assure you that the atmosphere was getting pretty hot with bullets and shells . . . but for all that he had no fear . . . about half a dozen German starlights shot up from one point on the right and a machine gun turned on. I said to him, 'You'd better keep low, sir!' but he never spoke and I dropped down on my stomach . . . The Captain dropped full on top of me and rolled on his side with his back to me. So I got on my knees and went round to the front of him and said, 'Are you hit, sir? Tell me where you are hit!' For a second he never spoke and then he said, 'Tell Mr. Porter to lead on with the company!' . . . Before two minutes he was gone (243)."

Fellow officers wrote to his parents, describing his courage. "We had a terrible time of it before we went over the top . . . the enemy was subjecting us to an intensive bombardment of gas shells and shrapnel . . . Yet your son kept wonderfully cool . . . When orders came through for our last move into the firing line . . . and the rest of us were pacing about restlessly, he took out a pocket edition of La Bruyere's 'Caractères' and continued to read it until we actually moved off . . . It is very certain that both his officers and men trusted him implicitly and would have followed him anywhere . . . (244)"

Those daily letters ceased. The Battle ground on. Gerard's last letter arrived posthumously.

"Dearest ones,

This is just a short note for you. We go into action in a day or two and I'm leaving this in case I don't come back. It brings you both . . . my very dearest love. Try not to grieve too much for me.

I hope my death will have been worthy of your trust and I couldn't die for a better cause . . . (245)"

The King and Queen, the Prime Minister, Sir John French all sent their condolences. J. L. Garvin himself wrote a long obituary of his son for his paper under the heading "One of the New Armies. A Noble Death."

"He was beloved by all that knew him, and with his fall at the age of twenty goes out a life of high promise. His colonel writes, 'I thought he would live to be a great man! . . . '

"Before the war . . . he had penned a defence of patriotism . . . He wrote, 'We would not willingly give up our reverence for the old splendours of our history, for the men who have conquered glory for England in Battle, who have won Empire for her, who have shed honour upon her by their work of whatever kind. And the discovery that after all we need have no misgivings about patriotism is one to touch deeper strings in our being than we would readily allow many others to see . . . '

"There . . . he unconsciously penned his own epitaph . . . From the age of ten, he seemed to know that when he grew up it would be to fight for Britain in a war of wars and there was sometimes that about him which suggested that . . . he had a steady intuition of his end. He was worthy of the New Armies and of The Cause. He would have desired no higher praise (246) ."

In a leading article in *The Observer*, Garvin took his son as a representative of all those thousands of other dead young soldiers. He used his last words, "Carry on," as a message to the nation to continue its war efforts.

"There is another word to say to many at home at a time when Britain has taken a sacrament of sorrow and when more homes are shadowed in the land than ever before . . . Two things must be remembered by a nation faithful to its dead. We cannot be true to them by mere endurance, no matter how stoical, nor by feeling, no matter how tender, but only by doing and acting. If we have lost anyone near to us, we try and live for two, so far as what remains of our own existence enables. There must be no apathy of repining. If Britain has lost so many young lives in whom resided incalculable possibilities of achievements, we who are left behind must seek the more to give every atom of our energy to the present and future needs of our country . . . ''

Garvin toured the Somme battlefields after the war to see the wasteland where his son died. "The old battlefields of the Somme, once a picture of lively hamlets, diligent homesteads, sleek cultivation, are now scenes of wild desolation more lonely and sinister than the witches' heath in *Macbeth*! No man who has ever traversed them can hope to tell what they are like, or what he felt there. (247)"

Garvin lived on to see the victory turned to ashes in a second greater war. Like many parents of the 1914–18 era, he knew the dreadful inversion of a world where the young died before the old. And, like thousands of other young men, his son went to join what Sassoon called:

> *The unreturning army that was youth;*
> *The legions who have suffered and are dust.*

Table of Dates

1914 28th June   Franz Ferdinand assassinated at Sarajevo.

28th July   Austria declares war on Serbia.

31st July   Russian mobilization of troops.

1st Aug.   Germany declares war on Russia.

2nd Aug.   German ultimatum to Belgium.

3rd Aug.   Germany declares war on France and invades Belgium.

4th Aug.   Britain declares war on Germany.

6th Aug.   Kitchener's appeal for volunteers for British "New Armies."

8th Aug.   British Expeditionary Force lands in France.

MAIN EVENTS INVOLVING BRITISH FORCES IN FRANCE

(Key turning points of the war in brackets)

1914 24th Aug.–5th Sept. Allied retreat from Mons.

5th–15th Sept.   Battle of the Marne. German retreat to the Aisne.

October   The "Race to the Sea."

17th–30th Oct.   First Battle of Ypres.

December   Western Front established.

1915 10th March   Battle of Neuve Chapelle.

April–May   Second Battle of Ypres. Germans use poison gas.

(23rd April   Italy enters war on Allied side).

(25th April)   Allied forces land at Gallipoli in effort to start New Front).

(June   First Zeppelin attacks on London).

25th Sept.–8th Oct. Battle of Loos.

4th Dec.   Chantilly Conference: Plans made for Allied Offensives in 1916.

16th Dec.   Sir Douglas Haig succeeds Sir John French as Commander of B.E.F.

(19th Dec.   Allied withdrawal from Gallipoli).

117

1916	21st Feb.	Battle of Verdun begins (continues until Dec. 1916).
	(31st May–1st June	Battle of Jutland: British naval domination secure).
	(4th June	Russian Brussilov offensive).

THE BATTLE OF THE SOMME

1916	24th–30th June	Somme Bombardment.
	1st July	Anglo-French assault begins: Initial disaster.
	14th July	Second major offensive: Bazentin Ridge night attack.
	July–August	Attrition fighting: Delville Wood/ Pozières.
	September	Capture of Ginchy and Guillemont.
	15th Sept.	Tanks first used at Flers-Courcelette Battle.
	25th Sept.	Morval and Combles fall.
	26th Sept.	Thiepval captured.
	October	Minor advances in the mud.
	13th–18th Nov.	Last attacks on the Ancre: Capture of Beaumont-Hamel.
1917	Feb.–March	German retreat to Hindenberg line.
	April	Battles of Arras and Vimy Ridge.
	(6th April	U.S.A. declares war on Germany).
	7th June	Battle of Messines.
	31st July–10th Nov.	Third Battle of Ypres: Passchendaele. Successful tank attack at Cambrai.
	(7th Nov.	Communists seize power in Russia.)
1918	21st March	German offensives break Western Front.
	July–August	Successful Allied counter-attacks: German retreat.
	Sept.–Nov.	Allied advance towards Germany.
	11th Nov.	End of the War: Armistice between Allies and Central Powers.

Leading Figures of the Somme Era

ASQUITH, HERBERT (1852–1928) British Liberal Politician. Prime Minister 1908–16. His son Raymond died in the Somme Battle.

CHURCHILL, WINSTON (1874–1965) First Lord of the Admiralty 1911–15. Dismissed Nov., 1915, after failure of Dardanelles/Gallipoli Campaign. Joined Army as Front Line Officer (Jan.–May, 1916). Shrewd critic of military policy. A tank pioneer himself, he joined Lloyd George's Ministry of Munitions in 1917 to produce tanks in thousands.

HAIG, DOUGLAS (1861–1928) British Field Marshal. Commander of B.E.F. Dec., 1915–Nov., 1918. Led battle failures of 1916–17 and victories of 1918.

KITCHENER, HORATIO (1850–1916) Distinguished for success as military commander in Sudan (1898) and South Africa (1900–02). Appointed Secretary of State for War August, 1914. Organized huge "New Armies" of volunteers. Lost with H.M.S. *Hampshire* 5th June, 1916.

LLOYD GEORGE, DAVID (1863–1945) Welsh Liberal Politician. Minister of Munitions 1915–16. Prime Minister 1916–22. His forceful policies made him "The Man who won the War."

RAWLINSON, HENRY (1864–1925) Commander Fourth Army in France to 1918. In charge of British attacks on Somme, 1916.

FALKENHAYN, ERICH VON (1861–1922) German General. Chief of General Staff (Dec., 1914–Aug., 1916). Planned attack on Verdun, 1916.

HINDENBERG, PAUL (1847–1934) German General recalled from retirement in 1914. Led German victories on Russian Front at Tannenberg (1914) and Masurian Lakes (1915). Appointed to lead German Armies on Western Front 1916.

LUDENDORFF, ERICH (1865–1937) German General. Shared

Hindenberg's career on Eastern and Western Fronts as his deputy.

JOFFRE, JOSEPH (1852–1931) French General. Commander-in-Chief of French Armies 1915. Carried out attrition war against German invaders. Removed from office and made Marshal of France 1916.

Acknowledgements

The publishers wish to thank the Hutchinson Publishing Group for permission to quote from Sylvia Pankhurst's *The Home Front*, published by Hutchinson in 1932, and Sidgewick & Jackson for permission to quote from Herbert Asquith's *Poems 1912–28* published by Sidgewick & Jackson in 1934. They also wish to thank Mrs. Susan Frankau for permission to quote from Gilbert Frankau's *The Guns*, published by Chatto & Windus in 1916; Robert Graves, for permission to quote eight lines from his poem "The Dead Boche" which appeared in his *Collected Poems 1914–1917*; G. T. Sassoon for permission to quote from Siegfried Sassoon's "Died of Wounds" which appeared in his *Collected Poems*; and to Methuen & Co., Ltd. for permission to quote from John Oxenham's poem, "The Nameless Grave," which appeared in *All's Well*. The song "Long, long trail" appeared in *The Long Trail: An Anthology of Soldiers' Songs* (Deutsch, 1965) and is used by kind permission of the authors, Eric Partridge and John Brophy. The Garvin family letters appear by kind permission of Mrs. K. Gordon.

Picture Credits

The publishers would like to thank the following for their kind permission to reproduce copyright illustrations on the pages mentioned: Trustees of the Imperial War Museum, jacket, 13 (bottom), 18, 21, 25, 28, 31, 35, 37, 38, 44, 46, 50, 52–53, 56, 58, 60, 74, 77, 79, 82, 84, 87, 88–89, 90, 98, 99, 100, 104–105, 116; *Daily Express*, frontispiece, 70; Radio-Times Hulton Picture Library, 8, 11, 15, 96; The Mansell Collection, 13 (top right), 69, 72, 93, 108; Trustees of the Victoria and Albert Museum, 13 (top left); Ben Uri Art Gallery (Hamlyn), 32; *Illustrated London News*, 63. The maps on pages 30 and 80 were drawn by Andrew Martin.

Notes on Sources

(1) B. H. Liddell-Hart, *History of the First World War* (Cassell, 1970)
(2) *Ibid*
(3) J. Galsworthy, *Daily News,* 31st Aug., 1914
(4) M. Macdonagh, *In London during the Great War* (Eyre & Spottiswoode, 1935)
(5) H. Asquith, *Poems 1912–28* (Sidgewick & Jackson, 1934)
(6) R. Brooke, *Collected Poems* (Sidgewick & Jackson, 1918)
(7) W. Churchill, *The World Crisis* (Butterworth, 1927)
(8) Macdonagh, *op. cit.*
(9) *Ibid*
(10) J. B. Priestley, *Margin Released* (Heinemann, (1962)
(11) I. Hay, *The First Hundred Thousand* (Blackwood, 1916)
(12) G. Coppard, *With a Machine Gun to Cambrai* (H.M.S.O., 1969)
(13) *Liverpool Daily Post,* Aug. 29, 1914
(14) V. Germains, *The Kitchener Armies* (Peter Davies, 1930)
(15) *Ibid*
(16) Macdonagh, *op. cit.*
(17) *Ibid*
(18) C. E. Montague, *Disenchantment* (Macgibbon & Kee, 1922)
(19) *Ibid*
(20) *The Nation,* 27th Dec., 1919
(21) quoted I. F. Clarke, *Voices Prophesying War* (Oxford, 1960)
(22) H. Williamson, *A Test to Destruction* (Macdonald, 1960)
(23) quoted by Liddell-Hart, *op. cit.*
(24) Churchill, *op. cit.*
(25) E. Blunden, *Undertones of War* (Oxford, 1956)
(26) H. Williamson, *A Patriot's Progress* (Macdonald, 1930)
(27) R. Aldington, *Death of a Hero* (Heinemann, 1929)
(28) Blunden, *op. cit.*
(29) P. Gibbs, *Realities of War* (Heinemann, 1920)
(30) quoted in *Anthology of Armageddon* (Denis Archer, 1935)
(31) R. Aldington, *op. cit.*
(32) H. Williamson, *How Dear is Life* (Macdonald, 1954)
(33) P. Wyndham-Lewis, *Blasting and Bombardiering* (Eyre & Spottiswoode, 1937)
(34) J. Masefield, *The Old Front Line* (Heinemann, 1917)
(35) *Ibid*
(36) P. Gibbs, *op. cit.*
(37) *Ibid*
(38) *Ibid*
(39) Blunden, *op. cit.*
(40) Coppard, *op. cit.*
(41) R. Graves, *Observer* article, 7th Nov., 1968
(42) Gibbs, *op. cit.*
(43) C. Carrington, *Soldier from the Wars Returning* (Hutchinson, 1965)
(44) R. Graves, *Goodbye to All That* (Cassell, 1929)
(45) Gibbs, *op. cit.*
(46) G. Frankau, *The Guns* (Chatto & Windus, 1916)
(47) H. M. Tomlinson, *All our Yesterdays* (Heinemann, 1930)
(48) Blunden, *op. cit.*
(49) H. Read, essay in *Promise of Greatness* (Cassell, 1968)
(50) R. Feilding, *War Letters to a Wife* (Medici, 1929)
(51) *The Nation,* 23rd Sept., 1916
(52) F. Manning, *Her Privates We* (Peter Davies, 1930)
(53) A. J. Taylor, *English History 1914–45* (Oxford, 1965)
(54) J. Brophy & E. Partridge, *The Long Trail* (A. Deutch, 1965)
(55) Blunden, *op. cit.*
(56) Graves, *op. cit.*
(57) R. H. Tawney, *The Nation,* 21st Oct., 1916
(58) Gibbs, *op. cit.*
(59) *Ibid*
(60) C. Lewis, *Sagittarius Rising* (Peter Davies, 1936)
(61) S. T. Coleridge, *Fears in Solitude* (1798)
(62) D. H. Lawrence, *Collected Letters* (Heinemann, 1962)
(63) quoted Graves, *op. cit.*
(64) S. Pankhurst, *The Home Front* (Hutchinson, 1932)
(65) Macdonagh, *op. cit.*

(66) *Ibid*
(67) quoted D. Mitchell, *Women on the Warpath* (Cape, 1966)
(68) quoted C. Playne, *Society at War* (Allen & Unwin, 1930)
(69) L. George, *War Memoirs* (Odhams, 1938)
(70) quoted Mitchell, *op. cit.*
(71) quoted D. Robinson, *The Zeppelin in Combat* (Foulis, 1962)
(72) D. H. Lawrence, *Kangaroo* (Heinemann, 1923)
(73) Macdonagh, *op. cit.*
(74) *Daily Express*, 13th Jan., 1916
(75) H. Bottomley, *Great Thoughts* (Holden & Hardingham, 1918)
(76) quoted D. Boulton, *Objection Overruled* (Macgibbon & Kee, 1967)
(77) The Bryce Commismission Report (H.M.S.O., 1915)
(78) *Daily Graphic*, 5th July, 1916
(79) *Daily Mail*, 22nd Sept., 1914
(80) "A Corpse Conversion Factory" pamphlet
(81) Bottomley, *op. cit.*
(82) Pankhurst, *op. cit.*
(83) L. Housman ed., *War Letters of Fallen Englishmen* (Gollancz, 1930)
(84) Gibbs, *op. cit.*
(85) R. Blake ed., *Private Papers of Douglas Haig* (Eyre & Spottiswoode, 1952)
(86) J. Edmonds, *British

Official History: Military operations France and Belgium 1916, Vol. I* (Macmillan, 1932)
(87) *Ibid*
(88) quoted A. H. Farrar-Hockley, *The Somme* (Batsford, 1964)
(89) quoted A. Horne, *Death of a Generation: The Somme and Verdun* (Macdonald, 1970)
(90) W. Griffith, *Up to Mametz* (Faber, 1931)
(91) J. Buchan, *The Battle of the Somme* (Nelson, 1916)
(92) *Ibid*
(93) Churchill, *op. cit.*
(94) Liddell-Hart, *op. cit.*
(95) quoted H. W. Wilson & J. A. Hammerton, *The Great War* (Amalgamated Press, 1914–19)
(96) Griffith, *op. cit.*
(97) D. Jones, *In Parenthesis* (Faber, 1937)
(98) Williamson, *The Golden Virgin* (Macdonald, 1957)
(99) Lewis, *op. cit.*
(100) quoted Farrar-Hockley, *op. cit.*
(101) appendix to *British Official History: Military Operations: France and Belgium 1916 Vol. II* (Macmillan, 1938)
(102) Housman ed., *op. cit.* (letter of 2 Lieut. A. Stephen)
(103) *Ibid* (letter of 2 Lieut. C. Carver)
(104) E. Blunden, *The Mind's Eye* (Cape, 1934)

(105) V. Brittain, *Testament of Youth* (Gollancz, 1933)
(106) Housman ed., *op. cit.* (letter of 2 Lieut. J. S. Engall)
(107) *Ibid* (letter of 2 Lieut. E. Polack)
(108) quoted Buchan, *op. cit.*
(109) G. Malins, *How I filmed the War* (Herbert Jenkins, 1920)
(110) *British Official History Vol. I, op. cit.*
(111) Gibbs, *op. cit.*
(112) *Malins, op. cit.*
(113) Housman ed., *op. cit.* (letter of 2 Lieut. W. B. Dyson)
(114) quoted Duff Cooper, *Haig* (Faber, 1935)
(115) *Ibid*
(116) Brittain, *op. cit.*
(117) W. N. Hodgson, *Verse and Prose in Peace and War* (Smith Elder Co. 1916)
(118) H. Williamson, *It was the Nightingale* (1958), *Love and the Loveless* (1962) (Macdonald)
(119) F. P. Crozier, *A Brass Hat in No-Man's Land* (Cape, 1930) —
(120) C. Lewis, *op. cit.*
(121) Housman ed., *op. cit.* (letter of 2 Lieut. A. Stephen)
(122) R. H. Tawney, *The Attack* (Allen & Unwin, 1953)
(123) J. Masefield, *The Battle of the Somme* (Heinemann, 1919)
(124) Malins, *op. cit.*
(125) Lewis, *op. cit.*
(126) Masefield, *Battle of the Somme*

(127) Tawney, *op. cit*
(128) M. Macdonagh, *The Irish on the Somme* (Hodder, 1917)
(129) S. Sassoon, *Memoirs of an Infantry Officer* (Faber, 1930)
(130) Carrington, *op. cit.*
(131) quoted Churchill, *op. cit.*
(132) H. Williamson, *The Wet Flanders Plain* (Beaumont Press, 1929)
(133) Macdonagh, *Irish on the Somme*
(134) Crozier, *op. cit.*
(135) Tawney, *op. cit.*
(136) Gibbs, *op. cit.*
(137) Tawney, *op. cit.*
(138) Masefield, *Battle of the Somme*
(139) Housman ed., *op. cit.* (letter of 2 Lieut. A. Stephen)
(140) quoted J. Harris, *The Somme: Death of a Generation* (Hodder, 1966)
(141) Gibbs, *op. cit.*
(142) E. L. Spears, *Liaison 1914* (Eyre & Spottiswood, 1930)
(143) *The Observer*, 2nd July, 1916
(144) *Ibid*
(145) *Daily Graphic*, 2nd July, 1916
(146) P. Gibbs, *The Battles of the Somme* (Heinemann, 1917)
(147) W. Beach-Thomas, *With the British on the Somme* (Methuen, 1917)
(148) A. J. Dawson, *Somme Battle Stories* (Hodder, 1916)
(149) *Daily Mail*, quoted *Illustrated London News*, 1916, Vol. II
(150) *Manchester Guardian*, 3rd July, 1916
(151) *Ibid*, 4th July, 1916
(152) *Ibid*
(153) C. S. Peel, *How We Lived Then* (Lane, 1929)
(154) quoted Farrar-Hockley, *op. cit.*
(155) Coppard, *op. cit.*
(156) G. Greenwell, *An Infant in Arms* (Allen Lane, the Penguin Press, 1971)
(157) G. Brennan, *A Life of One's Own* (Hamish Hamilton, 1962)
(158) Sassoon, *Memoirs of an Infantry Officer*
(159) Griffith, *op. cit.*
(160) Liddell-Hart, *op. cit.*
(161) M. Plowman, *A Subaltern on the Somme* (Dent, 1927)
(162) Gibbs, *Battles of the Somme*
(163) C. Carrington, *A Subaltern's War* (Peter Davies, 1929)
(164) C. E. W. Bean, *Australian Official History of the War*, Vol. II (Angus & Robertson, 1924)
(165) *Ibid*
(166) *Ibid*
(167) *Ibid*
(168) *Ibid*
(169) H. M. Tomlinson, *op. cit.*
(170) W. Ewart, *When Armageddon Came* (Cowan, 1933)
(171) Manning, *op. cit.*
(172) E. Blunden, essay in *Promise of Greatness* (Cassell, 1968)
(173) Lord Moran, *Anatomy of Courage* (Constable, 1945)
(174) Plowman, *op. cit.*
(175) Manning, *op. cit.*
(176) Churchill, *op. cit.*
(177) quoted Farrar-Hockley, *op. cit.*
(178) *Ibid*
(179) E. Ludendorff, *My War Memories, Vol. I* (Hutchinson, 1919)
(180) *Ibid*
(181) *The Nation*, 26th Aug., 1916
(182) *Cambridge Daily News*, 3rd Oct., 1916
(183) quoted B. H. Liddell-Hart, *The Tanks* (Cassell, 1959)
(184) Churchill, *op. cit.*
(185) E. Swinton, "Notes on the Employment of Tanks" (appendix to *British Official History, Vol. II* (France, 1916)
(186) *Ibid*
(187) George, *op. cit.*
(188) Housman ed., *op. cit.* (letter of Capt. T. M. Kettle)
(189) quoted B. Cooper, *The Ironclads of Cambrai* (Souvenir Press, 1967)
(190) W. Dival letter, quoted *Ibid*
(191) P. Gibbs, *War Despatches* (Gibbs & Phillips, 1966)
(192) Churchill, *op. cit.*
(193) Housman ed., *op. cit.* (Letter of 2 Lieut. A. Stephen)
(194) quoted Wilson & Hammerton, *op. cit.*
(195) Housman ed., *op. cit.* (letter of 2 Lieut. C.

Carver)

(196) A. D. Gristwood, *The Somme* (Portway Publications, 1927)

(197) *Ibid*

(198) Gibbs, *War Despatches*

(199) quoted Robinson, *The Zeppelin in Combat*

(200) Macdonagh, *In London during the Great War*

(201) *Ibid*

(202) S. Rogerson, *Twelve Days* (A. Barker, 1933)

(203) Plowman, *op. cit.*

(204) *Ibid*

(205) Greenwell, *op. cit.*

(206) Carrington, *Soldier from the Wars Returning*

(207) A. Hanbury-Sparrow, *The Land-locked Lake* (A. Barker, 1932)

(208) Blunden, *Undertones of War*

(209) *British Official History: Military operations France 1916, Vol. II*

(210) A. Hitler, *Mein Kampf* (Hurst & Blackett, 1939)

(211) Tomlinson, *op. cit.*

(212) L. Coulson, *From an outpost etc.* (Erskine Macdonald, 1917)

(213) R. Graves, "Dead Boche" in *Poems 1914–26* (Heinemann, 1926)

(214) S. Sassoon, "Died of Wounds" in *Selected Poems* (Faber, 1968)

(215) Sassoon, *Memoirs*

(216) B. Russell, *Justice in Wartime* (Open Court Publishing Co., 1916)

(217) *The Nation*, 7th Oct., 1916

(218) *Ibid*, 20th Dec., 1916

(219) quoted H. Asquith, *Memoirs and Reflections, Vol. II* (Cassell, 1932)

(220) Pankhurst, *op. cit.*

(221) Buchan, *op. cit.*

(222) quoted Playne, *op. cit.*

(223) J. Oxenham, *All's Well* (Methuen, 1916)

(224) Churchill, *op. cit.*

(225) Boraston ed., *Despatches of D. Haig* (Dent, 1919)

(226) Liddell-Hart, *op. cit.*

(227) Ludendorff, *op. cit.*

(228) Graves, *op. cit.*

(229) Jones, *op. cit.*

(230) *The Times*, 28th Aug., 1918

(231) H. Williamson, *Love and the Loveless*

(232) quoted E. Blunden, *Memoir of Wilfred Owen* (Chatto & Windus, 1931)

(233) Masefield. *op. cit.*

(234) *Ibid*

(235) *Ibid*

(236) W. Orpen, *An Onlooker in France* (Williams & Norgate, 1924)

(237) F. Scott Fitzgerald, *Tender is the Night* (New York, 1939)

(238) quoted R. Pound, *The Lost Generation* (Constable, 1969)

(239) *The Nation*, 23rd Sept., 1916

(240) Unpublished letter of G. Garvin

(241) Unpublished letter of G. Garvin

(242) Unpublished letter of J. L. Garvin

(243) Unpublished letter to J. L. Garvin

(244) Unpublished letter to J. L. Garvin

(245) Unpublished letter of G. Garvin

(246) *The Observer*, 30th July, 1916

(247) K. Garvin, *Memoir of J. L. Garvin* (Heinemann, 1948)

Further Reading

GENERAL BACKGROUND

B. H. Liddell-Hart, *History of the First World War* (Cassell, 1970; Pan, 1972)

A. J. P. Taylor, *The First World War: An Illustrated History* (Hamish Hamilton, 1963; Penguin, 1970)

M. Gilbert, *First World War Atlas* (Weidenfield & Nicolson, 1970)

R. Parkinson, *The Origins of World War One* (Wayland, 1970)

The History of the First World War (Part work Purnell/BPC, 1969–71)

A. Howarth, S. Davies, M. Mckay, M. Wainwright, *First World War (Resources pack)* (Longman, 1974)

THE BATTLE

A. H. Farrar-Hockley, *The Somme* (Batsford, 1964; Pan, 1966)

J. Masefield, *The Old Front Line* (Heinemann, 1917; Spurbooks, 1972)

M. Middlebrook, *The First Day of the Somme* (Allen Lane, 1971)

R. Tames, *The Somme 1916* (Jackdaw, Cape, 1972)

The Official History of the War: Military operations, France and Belgium, 1916, Vol. 5: J. Edmonds; Vol. 6: W. Miles (Macmillan, 1922–28)

ANTHOLOGIES

L. Housman ed., *War Letters of Fallen Englishmen* (Gollancz, 1930)

B. Gardner ed., *Up the Line to Death* (Methuen, 1964)

G. Chapman ed., *Vain Glory* (Cassell, 1968)

PERSONAL EXPERIENCES

R. Graves, *Goodbye to All That* (Cassell, 1929; Penguin, 1960)

S. Sassoon, *Memoirs of an Infantry Officer* (Faber, 1930)

F. Manning, *Her Privates We* (Peter Davies, 1930; Pan, 1967)
E. Blunden, *Undertones of War* (Oxford, 1971)
C. Edmonds, *A Subaltern's War* (Peter Davies 1929; Icon, 1964)
L. W. Griffith, *Up to Mametz* (Faber, 1931)
M. Plowman, *A Subaltern on the Somme* (Dent, 1927)
G. Coppard, *With a Machine Gun to Cambrai* (H.M.S.O., 1969)
J. Terraine ed., *General Jack's Diary* (Eyre & Spottiswoode, 1964)
D. Jones, *In Parenthesis* (Faber, 1937)
C. Carrington, *Soldier from the Wars Returning* (Arrow, 1970)
J. Brophy and E. Partridge, *The Long Trail* (Soldiers' Songs and Slang (A. Deutch, 1965; Sphere 1969)
R. H. Tawney, *The Attack and Other Essays* (Allen & Unwin, 1952)

NEW WEAPONS

H. A. N. Jones, *The War in the Air* (Oxford, 1922–28)
C. Lewis, *Sagittarius Rising* (Peter Davies, 1936; Corgi, 1969)
K. Munson, *Fighters 1914–19* (Blandford, 1968)
B. H. Liddell-Hart, *The Tanks* (Cassell, 1959)

HOME FRONT

A. Marwick, *The Deluge* (Bodley Head, 1965; Penguin, 1967)
J. Williams, *The Home Fronts 1914–18* (Constable, 1972)
M. Macdonagh, *In London During the Great War* (Eyre & Spottiswoode, 1935)
M. Rickards, *Posters of the First World War* (Adams & Dart, 1968)

The Imperial War Museum (Lambeth Road, London S.E.1) publish posters, postcards and photopacks concerned with the 1914–18 war.

Index

RECORD OF BORROWERS
IMPORTANT